Waking the Slumbering Spirit

Dedicated to

Barbara Jean Bowman

October 23, 1942 - June 9, 1993

Through a wonderfully awakened personal spirit
Barbara blessed everyone she met
with love, encouragement,
hospitality, ministry,
prayer, and sharing
of the good news
of salvation through
Jesus Christ.

Waking the Slumbering Spirit

John and Paula
SANDFORD

Edited and expanded
by
Norm Bowman

Keys of Knowledge Series

Waking the Slumbering Spirit

John and Paula Sandford are founders of Elijah House, Inc., Christian ministries with headquarters in Post Falls, Idaho. They are veteran counselors, recognized internationally as teachers and authors in the field of family renewal and inner healing.

Elijah House, Inc.
S. 1000 Richards Road
Post Falls, Idaho 83854
Phone (208) 773-1645

Norm Bowman, Paula Sandford's brother, is president of Clear Stream Publishing in Arlington, Texas. A graduate of William Jewell College and New Orleans Baptist Theological Seminary, Norm is a former magazine editor with the Sunday School Board of the Southern Baptist Convention in Nashville, Tennessee.

Cover design and photography by Norm Bowman.

ISBN 0-9637741-0-7

Clear Stream, Inc. Publishing

Box 122128, Arlington, Texas 76012

Contents

Prelude

Understanding the Personal Spirit

Characteristics of an Awakened Spirit

Spiritual Therapy - Waking the Spirit

Postlude

What's Different
About This Book?

For many years now the focus of Elijah House has been on a ministry of restoration and reconciliation to born again Christians who are in need of inner healing and transformation. Most of our writing and teaching have been directed toward training both professional and lay counselors, to equip them to deal with the deep wounds and spiritual needs in the persons to whom they minister.

Our published works have often been used as text books by colleges and seminaries as they train men and women for ministry in the field of counseling and pastoral care. The comprehensive nature of these books has served that purpose well.

However, in recent years, we have been encouraged by many friends and co-workers to adapt our writing to a broader and less academic audience—to deal in more depth with specific teachings and to directly address the needs of lay persons, counselees, and small groups, rather than the professional counselor or clergy person.

Because of our busy traveling and teaching schedule, we have not been able to undertake this new writing task by ourselves. Consequently, we called on Norm Bowman to apply his considerable gifts as editor and writer to help us launch this project as co-author. **Waking the Slumbering Spirit** is the result. It is the first release of a group of topical books in the **Keys of Knowledge Series.** Norm has very effectively assimilated material from our books, lectures, tapes, and personal conversations to produce an entirely new work that, to our satisfaction, is exactly on target.

Books in the **Keys of Knowledge Series** are written for thinking Christians who are seeking spiritual growth and healing which will enrich their relationships with others and with God. All books include study guides at the end of each chapter to encourage self evaluation, small group interaction, and realistic "Life Applications."

We are confident that books in the **Keys of Knowledge Series** will prove to be powerful study guides and sources of help for fellowship groups, Sunday School classes, home Bible studies, and discipleship training groups as Christians attempt to uplift and nurture each other as fellow pilgrims along the way. Please let us hear from you through Elijah House so we can know how we have done.

John and Paula Sandford

Chapter 1
Sleepwalking in the Spirit

Ten year old Matthew grew increasingly concerned about the slender tabby who had been showing up each evening at the kitchen door. She would sit nervously on the porch step, staring into the house in hope that we would feed the other cats outside and there would be food left in their bowls. Waiting impatiently in the cold night air, she would stare at us through the storm door with big green eyes reflecting the warm light from within the house. If we approached to get a better look, she would retreat into the shadows. When we would take her a fresh bowl of food, she would run away and hide until the glass door once again separated us and she could safely come to eat.

Matthew named our timid visitor Fraidie, short for fraidie-cat. He tried his best to coax her into friendliness with sweet talk and food offered in his outstretched hand. But Fraidie was wild and would not respond. Born somewhere under a house or in a neighborhood shed, she had never experienced the taming effect of human touch. She grew up wary and afraid, living a tenuous life of scavenging at our back door and making a bad weather home in our garage by climbing through one of the windows Matt had kicked out with his soccer ball.

Some months later the inevitable happened and Fraidie became a mother in our garage. We had suspected as much but nevertheless were surprised one Saturday morning to see a fat waddling ball of fur scurrying behind some boxes and old bicycles in the dark garage. A thorough search produced one kitten that had not survived, and a cute and very frightened little female that we decided had to be rescued from the kind of life her mother was leading.

We brought the nearly weaned baby inside and after a few days of eyedropper milk-feedings she made the transition to solid food. The weeks that followed were filled with real wonder. The scared and trembling kitten quickly warmed to being held and touched. By day she would frolic and play for hours with Matthew on the floor. By night she would snuggle up against our seventeen-year-old blind and deaf poodle—getting warmth and comfort from a surrogate canine mom.

No longer an untouchable fraidie-cat, doomed to a life of lonely scavenging, the kitten quickly took her place as a full member of the family. She became wonderfully alive in her spirit, playfully affectionate, and flourishing in every way as she grew. In touching tribute to her mother, Matthew named the kitten Lady—a name to rhyme with Fraidie, but so distinctly different.

What has this story to do with the slumbering spirit? Begin by trying to understand it as a kind of parable and open your spiritual ears to hear. God has so much to reveal to those who will listen and for those who can open their hearts to His continuing words of instruction on how to become more fully human.

Fraidie-cat's baby became Lady the family member because she came into the proper kind of loving nurture; a nurture that transformed her from a wild creature to a loving pet. That message, translated into human development, is a prophetic message from God. Our world is sadly lacking in similar loving nurture that could produce fully functional adults with alive and responsive personal spirits. Knowing what to do about this problem begins with recognizing that the problem exists.

Sounding an alarm to arouse slumbering spirits is as much a prophetic task as that of the old testament prophets in calling Israel back into proper relationship with God.

Keys of Knowledge

The role of the prophet is to deliver the word of God to His people. The prophet admonishes, warns, directs, intercedes, teaches, and counsels. He stands at the walls to see what the

Lord is doing so that he might call the body of Christ to respond appropriately.

Some may suggest that as a result of the mission and ministry of Jesus, God did away with prophets and prophecy because they were no longer needed. But this is not so. Instead, God has expanded the prophet's function and power, by virtue of what Jesus accomplished on the cross and through His resurrection. The prophet should no longer be conceived of as the lonely watchman on the wall of his culture.

God has redirected that role so the prophet can now be an integral part of the church whose role is to carry on the work of Christ in bringing the world into rightful relationship with God. The church, through the guidance of the Holy Spirit, should cherish the prophetic role and protect its prophets, giving them support structures to more effectively reach His people in need of God's Word.

One of the important functions of that prophetic role is to interpret to the people God's "keys of knowledge" so they might come into closer relationship and greater freedom with their Lord.

"Woe to you experts in the law, because you have taken away the key to knowledge. You yourselves have not entered and you have hindered those who were entering." (Luke 11: 52)

Life is complex. Even though we strive to seek God's leadership, it is not easy to make our way in this world with a sense of God-directed purpose. When value systems get confused and when sin and circumstances entrap us, we need the clarity of God's vision to find our way and to be set free to live as He would like us to live. Prophets provide the keys of knowledge for that clarity of vision.

Unfortunately, institutionalization of religion and strict adherence to laws and rituals have always served as obstacles to the spiritual freedom God wants us to achieve. In the time of Christ, the Pharisees were very zealous in their attempts to promote righteousness among the people. But Jesus condemned them because even when they were not hypocritical they tended to *"load people down with burdens they can hardly carry." (Luke 11: 46)*

God does not want to load us down with hopeless burdens of behavioral laws. While God's laws are always to be obeyed, repressive human additions to morals and misapplied guilt are often major factors in sabotaging the freedom that should come with the experience of rebirth in Jesus Christ. What we all need are keys of knowledge that will help us to understand where we are and why we are in the condition we are in. We need to meet our Lord in a very personal way and unlock our deepest beings to live in the spirit and the truth of God. We need to be awakened to the wonder of Jesus Christ living in us and bringing us into the fullness of our humanity.

For most people in the world today, God's keys of knowledge are lost in a sea of ambiguity. Our contemporary culture deafens us with the noise of conflicting values and ideologies. People have no sense of certainty on which to anchor their lives and to establish priorities.

The Lord sent us into this ministry a long time ago as prophets; working at first in the pastorate, then founding the Elijah House center for counseling, and subsequently in a teaching and writing ministry that has stretched around the world. During our many years of counseling, thousands of people have come to us to seek ways to put their shattered lives back together.

During these years of listening to both the hurts of men and women and to the voice of God, we have been given a number of keys of knowledge to interpret to the church. These include:

The Slumbering Spirit

A slumbering spirit can be caused in two ways. Poor nurture in childhood causes the personal spirit to be stunted just as a flower is stunted without proper nutrients. In adulthood, the personal spirit can also fall asleep through neglect of prayer and devotional life; by withdrawing from intimacy with others; by falling into repeated sin; and/or by ceasing to participate in the wonders of recreational fun, nature, art, and music.

A slumbering spirit results in the crippling of one's ability to function in many areas of daily living. Among these consequences are a lack of a true conscience; inability to communicate intimately and to sustain close relationships; inability to worship and have a fulfilling devotional life; inability to learn from the past or project into the future; and inability to sustain good health. Persons slumbering in spirit are usually unaware there is so much more depth to life than they are experiencing.

Performance Orientation

One of the most common maladies throughout the world, performance orientation consists of a pervasive need to please others and perform up to the expectations of others. This means striving to perform for wrong motives—to win love and a sense of belonging when those have already been given. The result can be a compulsive work ethic, preoccupation with doing everything right, an inordinate desire to be liked or approved of, and dissatisfaction with yourself for what you have *achieved* as opposed to who you *are* as a person. In Christians, it is rooted in an inability to believe God can love us unless we work for it.

Bitter Root Judgment and Expectancy

A surprising consequence can develop by making judgments and harboring ill will toward parents or others with whom you have significant relationships. Judgments can turn inward as bitter roots and produce the same behavioral tendencies in yourself that you found hurtful and destructive from others! You unknowingly act out your own judgments. You come to expect things to be a certain way and consequently they always seem to turn out the way you expect them to. This causes you to reap by immutable law the results of what you have sown in judgments.

Inner Vows

When you experience hurt in your childhood, a common re-action is to employ an emotional self defense by making an inner vow that you will never let yourself be vulnerable in that way again. This emotional barrier can shut you off from fulfilling relationships because your inner self will never let go enough to trust and risk in vulnerability.

Heart of Stone

Years of neglect or hurt can cause emotional callousness to develop, protecting the inner person from further hurt by stifling real feelings, avoiding vulnerability, blocking out tenderness, and refusing to listen or be sensitive to the needs of others. This is often characterized by rugged individualism born of cynicism, resulting in emotional impenetrability.

Wounded Burden Bearers

As loving and sensitive people, we rejoice and grieve constantly as we live among our neighbors. There is danger in burden bearing because if not properly handled, it can wound your spirit and drain you of life. But when burdens are properly carried through intercessory prayer and by being in touch with refreshment from the Lord, burden bearing is the key to fullness of life. In the most positive sense, burden bearers are those who consciously seek out the hurts of others in order to transmit those hurts to the Lord for healing.

Books in the **Keys of Knowledge Series** explore how inner healing is produced through repentance, forgiveness, and transformation through Christian love.

Waking the Slumbering Spirit portrays how a slumbering personal spirit can be diagnosed and suggests many ways in which Christians can overcome this debilitating condition in their lives. A number of important terms will be defined in this first chapter. Later chapters will then describe why the spirit slumbers, illustrate characteristics of an awakened spirit, and suggest ways to keep a child's spirit awake or to reawaken the spirit of a slumbering adult.

Understanding the Slumbering Spirit

An understanding of the slumbering spirit is a powerful and incisive key of knowledge God has given us to help set people free. This concept was discovered the hard way by struggling unsuccessfully to help many people over the years through counseling. A number of people seemingly could not experience a breakthrough of healing and growth in their lives.

Although we applied every counseling technique and every intellectual and spiritual resource we knew of, it seemed they just could not break away from ingrained patterns of destructive attitudes and behavior. They sincerely came looking for help and were willing to try whatever we would suggest. But they could not function in some areas of life essential for personal growth and in sustaining healthy relationships with others.

We had been particularly puzzled because many of these counselees seemed to be equipped better than most with the resources needed to succeed in life. One might describe them as born-anew, Bible-believing, church-attending Christians who attempted to love and serve others. But in some areas of their being, it was as though cogs were missing. Their behavior proved to be erratic and unpredictable, and they would surprise everyone regularly with decisions and actions that contradicted their professed beliefs as Christians.

Many of these people seemed incapable of understanding cause and effect relationships. They couldn't make the connection that certain patterns of behavior produce predictably destructive consequences for themselves and others. Characteristically, they lived only for the moment and appeared incapable of avoiding the kind of decisions that would invariably get them into trouble and wound the lives and spirits of their loved ones.

A striking example of this was a young man who came to us for counseling with his wife. He seemed to have everything going for him. He clearly loved his wife and children. As a member of a charismatic church, he was Holy Spirit-filled, Bible-believing, and active in church activities. But he was always getting into trouble because he would not pay his bills. He would buy things on credit and then neglect to make payments when the bills came due. When creditors would call, he would become absolutely furious because he felt they had no right to bother him! He seemed to have no awareness or conscience about what not paying his bills did to other people.

Every once in a while he would also become sexually involved with other women with no apparent conscience about the morality of his behavior. He had no sense that his adulterous actions would wound the heart of the Lord, or wound his wife and his relationship with his family. After many frustrating counseling sessions, he had us crying out to God: "What's the matter here! Why doesn't this guy take responsibility for paying his bills? Why doesn't he seem to have a conscience about his immoral behavior?"

During this same period of time we were traveling a great deal, often crossing trails with some well-known evangelists and preachers who were holding services in churches across the country. In our conversations with church people in those local communities, we were surprised to learn that several of these religious celebrities had reputations as womanizers, becoming sexually involved with women in almost every community they visited. The result, of course, was a great deal of anguish and hurt among the church people in those communities, and disillusionment among the fragile new believers who had been moved to faith by these representatives of God.

We found ourselves again crying out to God: "How can this be? How can men like this, who really believe in and self-sacrificially serve the Lord, fail to possess a moral conscience about what they do? How can they allow their Christian witness to be so jeopardized by their immoral actions?"

Concerning this matter of men and women of God acting in un-godly ways, you need to understand that the gifts and the calling of God are permanent.

"For God's gifts and his call are irrevocable."
(Romans 11: 29) (NAS)

That is to say, when God gives a gift or a calling He doesn't take it back. When a person works a miracle through God's power, it says nothing about the character of the person. It speaks of the character of God.

That is a very difficult concept for some people to understand, because we often attribute more importance to the personality of the message bearer than to the content and power of the message itself. We are not saved or healed by a preacher; we are saved or healed by the power of God. The preacher is just the instrument through which the Holy Spirit works to reach us. God can work perfect miracles through rascals, and He often does.

The validity of your baptism does not depend on the righteousness of the priest or pastor who baptized you. Your baptism is between you and God. The power of the sacrament is dependent solely on God's grace. Similarly, the oneness you experience with Jesus Christ through communion is not dependent on whether the minister who serves you happens to be righteous. He may be a rascal, but the communion is perfectly valid because God vindicates the position. God acts anyway.

The fact that a man works miracles doesn't mean that his own life is righteous. Men do not cause miracles to happen, and they should not be revered as though they have that power. It is God who performs miracles, and He sometimes chooses to do it through those who may seem unworthy by our earthly standards.

Confused, hurt, and disappointed about Christians who seemed to live with no conscience, we asked God for an answer in what by that time had become our fervent prayer: we simply cried "HELP!" God heard our cry and answered.

The answer God revealed was this: These persons have never had awakened personal spirits. Their spirits are slumbering.

Questions immediately came to mind: What does "slumbering spirit" mean? Where and in what way is "slumbering spirit" spoken of in the Scriptures?

The Lord further revealed that if someone has a slumbering spirit, he or she becomes incapable of functioning adequately in those areas of life in which the spirit affects people at the deepest level. Among these are the conscience, building and sustaining personal relationships, intimate communication, and devotional life. The mind still works. Emotions still work. But the spirit is dysfunctional because it is in a sleep state. By looking more closely at the Scriptures we saw many references to the slumbering spirit that we had never been aware of before.

"But everything exposed by the light becomes visible, for it is light that makes everything visible. This is why it is said: Wake up, O sleeper, rise from the dead, and Christ will shine on you."(Ephesians 5: 13)

We had read this Bible passage many times before, with the perception that these fledgling Ephesian Christians were simply being admonished by Paul to get serious, try harder, and put their immorality behind them. But on closer look, we saw much more. These were slumbering spirits—Christian believers so entrapped in their life-style that Paul likened them to zombies who needed to be awakened from the dead so the light of Christ might shine on them.

Whether stunted in the spirit from lack of loving nurture as children, or falling into sleep as adults through sin, fleeing from affection, and neglecting worship and prayer, the effects are the same.

The spirit becomes locked in a shadowy world
of unawareness. The mind and emotions may be awake,
but the person is sleepwalking in the spirit.

Escaping from this trap of darkness is not accomplished by the intellectual act of saying, "I believe," or even by working very hard at being a moral person. The spirit must be awakened and re-nurtured through committed discipleship and the patient love of friends and family.

Awakening must begin with awareness of the slumbering state you find yourself in. The awakening grows as you learn new behaviors such as Paul catalogs in the fifth chapter of Ephesians. As these new ways are learned, the spirit will awaken and the light of Jesus Christ will shine on and through you.

- Be careful and choose wisely how you will live.
- Find out what pleases the Lord and be imitators of Christ.
- Stay away from intoxicants that drug your senses and make you susceptible to immorality.
- Seek opportunities for lightheartedness, with laughter, singing, and spirit-filled fun.
- Give thanks to God for everything life brings.
- Submit to each other in love and trust as Christian brothers and sisters.
- Be honorable in your family relationships, treating others with respect and consideration.
- Seek the Lord for strength, nourishing, and cherishing. Be confident in His power to nurture and protect you.

In the months following, our prayers were answered as our search of the Scriptures continued to reveal truths about the slumbering spirit. The personal spirit slumbers in the life of so many people. Many in Christ's church, even leaders, are like dreamers.

"Israel's watchmen are blind, they all lack knowledge; they are all mute dogs, they cannot bark; they lie around and dream, they love to sleep." (Isaiah 56: 10)

"The hour has come for you to wake up from your slumber, because our salvation is nearer now than when we first believed. The night is nearly over; the day is almost here. So let us put aside the deeds of darkness and put on the armor of light. Let us behave decently, as in the daytime, not in orgies and drunkenness, not in sexual immorality and debauchery, not in dissension and jealousy. Rather, clothe yourself with the Lord Jesus Christ, and do not think about how to gratify the desires of the sinful nature." (Romans 13: 11-14)

Please understand here, that if our spirits are awake, we put on Jesus and walk in Jesus' nature. If our spirits fall asleep, we put on the flesh and walk in the flesh.

"Awake, awake, O Zion, clothe yourself with strength. Put on your garments of splendor, O Jerusalem, the holy city. The uncircumcised and defiled will not enter you again. Shake off your dust; rise up, sit enthroned, O Jerusalem. Free yourself from the chains on your neck, O captive daughter of Zion." (Isaiah 52: 1-2)

"But you brothers are not in darkness so that this day should surprise you like a thief. You are all sons of the light and sons of the day. We do not belong to the night or to the darkness. So

then, let us not be like others, who are asleep, but let us be alert and self-controlled." (I Thessalonians 5: 4-6)

Can you imagine the Church with a grand case of insomnia, trying to stay awake until the Lord comes? Paul isn't talking about physical sleep, is he? He is talking about spiritual slumber.

"Behold, I come like a thief! Blessed is he who stays awake and keeps his clothes with him, so that he may not go naked and be shamefully exposed." (Revelation 16: 15)

You see that when we fall asleep spiritually, we lose the garments of Jesus Christ, and walk about in the shame of our flesh.

With this newfound key of knowledge of the slumbering spirit fresh in our minds, we went out into the body of Christ to teach from our awareness. But to our chagrin, we found that most people had little or no understanding of the specific functions of the personal spirit. We found ourselves needing to explain what the personal spirit is as contrasted to the:

- Functions of the soul
- Thoughts and emotions of our minds
- Inter-relatedness of our bodies to spirit, mind and soul

This was true of nearly everyone, including those in the church as well as those out in the secular world. In order to more fully understand what it means to have a slumbering spirit, let's begin with some basic definitions of those elements which make up our being:

- Personal Spirit
- Soul
- Mind
- Body

Our Personal Spirits

The root meaning of both the Hebrew and Greek words for spirit is a movement of air, or wind.

"The Spirit of God was moving over the face of the waters." (Genesis 1: 2b)

The spirit is the life principle or energy of all life. Our personal spirit is that which God has breathed into us from the beginning.

"The Lord God formed man from the dust of the ground and breathed into his nostrils the breath of life, and the man became a living being." (Genesis 2: 7)

Jesus said to Nicodemus:
"Flesh gives birth to flesh but the Spirit gives birth to spirit. You must not be surprised at my saying, you must be born again. The wind blows wherever it pleases. You hear the sound but you cannot tell where it comes from or where it is going. So it is with everyone born of the Spirit." (John 3: 8)

This passage reflects a play on words since the Greek word used can be translated both as wind and as spirit. Genesis 1:27 tells us that man is created in the image of God, meaning that man is like God by nature. We can take this to indicate that man has intelligence, free will, and is a moral being. From a Christian point of view, being in God's image indicates the possibility for mankind to be transformed into the personality of Christ.

"For those God foreknew he also predestined to be conformed to the likeness of his Son, that he might be the firstborn among many brothers." (Romans 8: 29)

"And we, who with unveiled faces all reflect the Lord's glory, are being transformed into his likeness with ever increasing glory, which comes from the Lord, who is the Spirit." (2 Corinthians 3: 18)

The image of man in Hebrew thought was much less complex than New Testament thinking, which provides a more expansive view of spirit and soul. Paul wrote to a people versed in Greek philosophy and he attempted to combat their dualistic concept that the spirit and the body are separate—the spirit being good and the body evil.

In Hebrew thinking there was no separation of the soul into body, heart (mind), and spirit. The soul was the body, and one reasoned from one's heart. Wisdom, insight, inspiration, and courage came from the presence of God's Spirit. This spiritual nature of man to the Hebrew people was perceived in terms of their covenant relationship with God who would be present with them if they proved to be faithful to His will.

As Paul interpreted man and God to the more philosophical Greek culture of the first century, he portrayed what might be viewed as a triangle of personality in each of us:

♦ Mind (comprised of our will and our reason).

♦ Flesh (a term sometimes referring to our body, but used by Paul to mean selfish desire and bodily lusts.) We commonly strive to restrain our "flesh" through law.

♦ Spirit (the precious life energy breathed into us by God).

Paul taught that these functions of our being are inseparably linked and are likely to do battle with each other until our spirit is renewed and we are transformed into the likeness of Christ. Our selfish desires can only be overcome through the power of God's grace. Then the mind and flesh are brought into harmony with Christ's will.

Paul portrays the spirit of man as that through which the Holy Spirit of God can indwell a person. The Spirit comforts, protects, inspires, and equips one with spiritual gifts to do God's reconciling work in the world. Our personal spirit is eternal. It will return to God, the Scripture says, and the body will return to dust. (Ecclesiastes 12: 7)

The most beautiful image imaginable is Jesus, through His Holy Spirit, standing at our spirit's door and knocking. Are we awake enough to hear, to rejoice, and to thankfully open the door and journey with Him? Or, do we sleep, unaware of the wonderful life He has prepared for us?

Our Souls

In Genesis 2:7 Scripture speaks of God breathing the breath of life (the spirit) into man and man becoming a living being (or soul). In many ways the words "spirit" and "soul" are used interchangeably in Scripture to refer to the life-principle or life-energy. A Hebrew would not speak of himself as having a body. Rather, he would speak in terms of being a soul (an animated psychophysical being in flesh form).

To portray the life-energy within a person, the term spirit was most often used. Unusual energy, skill, or inspiration were usually attributed to the presence of the Spirit of God. On the other hand, the term soul was most often used to refer to desire, appetite, or emotional experiences. The soul hungers and thirsts. The soul is satisfied, or feels joy, sorrow, hope, or despair.

As Christians, we can define the soul in general terms as that structure of the heart, mind, character, and personality which we build. We build the soul as our spirit encounters life, reacts, and develops coping mechanisms. The soul is the expression of our personality with which we make our way in the world. At times, it can be a temple through which our spirit finds beautiful expression. At other times, our soul can be a self-imposed prison of hatred, despair, resentment, or lust. And on still other occasions, our soul can be a battle tank in which we seek refuge while aggressively attacking outsiders who are considered to be a threat.

Our Minds

The mind is our intellect, our decision-making capability, our reasoning and logical self that chooses a course of action. In ancient Hebrew thought, the seat of intellect was considered to be the heart. However, the thinking heart (intellect) was more practical than speculative. Thoughts moved to action. They were not for doing battle in the realm of conflicting logic, as would be the case in New Testament times and even more so today.

In New Testament terminology, the mind is identified as one's reasoning capacity, often in tension with one's feelings or flesh. Our mind is subject to bad judgment and foolish decisions, and yet capable of transformation into harmony with one's God-directed spirit.

Many new age thinkers today elevate intellect to god-like status, referring to the "Universal Mind" as being the God-force itself in which we all share a mystical and synergistic destiny. However, New Testament revelations in the writings of Paul speak of an all-powerful and personal God who is in full control of His creation. God is the loving Creator/Father who has made provision for man to be brought into loving relationship.

Our mind is a God-given gift of intelligence and free choice which we can opt to squander or to invest. The mind is an integral part of our being. Our mind, in combination with our body, soul, and spirit, can be brought into harmony with God's will.

Our Bodies

At first thought it may seem foolish to construct a definition of the human body since we seem to be so familiar with our own flesh and blood. But in familiarity, we may have allowed ourselves to become overly simplistic in our perception of what our bodies are. The scientific community is in virtual agreement that we have only now begun to scratch the surface of understanding the mysteries of how the human body operates. From a physical standpoint, our bodies are incredible machines. But our bodies are so much more than chemistry and physics. There is an interrelatedness of body and spirit that cannot be measured in laboratory experiments.

When we abuse our bodies through overwork, stress, fatigue, diet, drugs, and poor hygiene, we suffer more than physical consequences. Our body "on tilt" affects our entire system. We are unable to think clearly. Our judgment is impaired. We become emotionally volatile. Depression sets in. We go into spiritual turmoil.

We are, in fact, much as the ancient Hebrews assumed us to be—an inseparable unity of spirit, soul, mind, and body. To understand this unity is to more clearly understand what the Scripture says in reference to our bodies as holy temples.

The Personal Spirit and the Holy Spirit

Some have asked what the relationship is between our personal spirit and the Holy Spirit. Does being filled with the Holy Spirit automatically cause an awakening of the personal spirit?

This question can be answered in a more perceptive way by stepping back and defining several terms frequently used in Christian circles, but misunderstood by many. These terms are:

- ♦ Evangelical
- ♦ Charismatic
- ♦ Pentecostal
- ♦ Spiritual Gifts
- ♦ Fruits of the Spirit
- ♦ Speaking in Tongues

A discussion of each of these could certainly fill a book of its own, and you can find ample reference material to do a full study on each of these areas if you wish. These issues are addressed here in order to clarify how the Holy Spirit impacts the life of individual Christians, how the role of the Holy Spirit is interpreted in different church groups, and the relationship this has to an awakened personal spirit.

Evangelical refers to those Christian people who know, have experienced, and teach what it is to be born anew—to receive Jesus as Lord and Savior.

Charismatic describes those who know and have experienced that rebirth in Jesus Christ, but also know what it is to have the Holy Spirit released within them. This means the purposeful use of spiritual gifts in one's life as tools of ministry.

The theological understanding of the Holy Spirit's presence has changed in recent years. There was a time when it was thought that if persons were not "filled with the Holy Spirit" (exercising gifts), then they did not yet have the Spirit present in them. However, we must remember that we have a triune God who is three in one, and whose personalities cannot be separated one from another. God and Jesus cannot come into one's life in a rebirth experience without the Holy Spirit as part of that event.

We now understand that the baptism of the Holy Spirit is a further release of the Holy Spirit who is already present, so that the Spirit can operate with power within the believer. A charismatic is one who understands and releases the spiritual gifts within his life. Spiritual gifts are given to equip the individual Christian for ministry and for the edification of the body of Christ.

Pentecostal refers to those old-line charismatics who first came into the "fullness of the Spirit." Generally, it refers to people who are more emotional, and who probably will profess the doctrine that if you haven't spoken in tongues you haven't "got" the spirit. Pentecostals tend to think of the Holy Spirit as working upon the person to cause the person to act in ways that he or she would not ordinarily act.

Too often, old line Pentecostals are those who may have spoken in tongues only once. They tend to think that speaking in tongues is something that happens to you, and never really understand that one who has the gift of tongues can speak in tongues at any time he or she wants.

"If anyone speaks in a tongue, two—or at the most— three should speak, one at a time, and someone must interpret." (1 Corinthians 14: 27)

In contrast, charismatics understand incarnation — that the Holy Spirit works in and through who you naturally are. Ideally, a charismatic Christian understands that we hold our gifts in earthen vessels and that we are responsible for the ways in which those gifts are exercised.

Spiritual Gifts refer to the special power given by God through the Holy Spirit to each individual, equipping a person in special ways to do God's work in the world for the edification of the church.

We have not been given a definitive list of spiritual gifts in the New Testament, but they are enumerated in the context of several of Paul's letters to the early churches. Depending on how one interprets his applications, the spiritual gifts include:

- ◆ **Apostleship**—One who applies cross-cultural adaptation for missionary purposes to found churches and to inspire great movements of Christian discipleship. *(1 Corinthians 12: 28)*

- ◆ **Wisdom**—Divine insight of how to apply biblical principles to difficult issues in life. *(1 Corinthians 12: 8)*

- ◆ **Knowledge**—The ability to uncover great principles of God's Word through study and research, and ability to know facts unaided by any other means than spiritual revelation. *(1 Corinthians 12: 8)*

- ◆ **Faith**—The ability to see God's purpose and to trust His wisdom and power to accomplish what seems impossible. *(1 Corinthians 12: 9)*

- **Healing and Miracles**—The ability to be an instrument of God's power to accomplish spiritual and physical healing and other miracles. *(1 Corinthians 12: 9-10)*

- **Prophecy**—The ability to understand and communicate God's Word with power, conviction and clarity. *(1 Corinthians 12: 10)*

- **Discernment**—The capacity to differentiate truth from error, or whether teachings originate from God, man, or Satan; and the ability to discern the presence of demons in or influencing people. *(1 Corinthians 12: 10)*

- **Speaking in Tongues**—The ability to praise God in the Spirit or to receive messages from God, Spirit to spirit. *(1 Corinthians 12: 10)*

- **Interpretation of Tongues**—The ability to interpret in a known language a message received from God through one speaking in tongues. *(1 Corinthians 12: 10)*

- **Teaching**—The unusual facility to grasp and communicate God's truth so others can clearly understand. *(1 Corinthians 12: 28; Romans 12: 7)*

- **Service**—The gift of recognizing needs and meeting them by giving of oneself joyfully and efficiently. *(1 Corinthians 12: 28; Romans 12: 7; 1 Peter 4: 10-11)*

- **Administration**—The ability to efficiently organize people and resources to accomplish God's specific goals. *(1 Corinthians 12: 28)*

- **Evangelism**—The desire and capacity to effectively share the gospel with others and bring them into saving faith in Christ. *(Ephesians 4: 11; Acts 21: 8)*

- **Exhortation**—The gift of counseling and encouraging others to become all that God wants them to be. *(Romans 12: 8)*

- ◆ **Leadership**—The ability to clearly see what must be done to accomplish God's work, and to inspire others to cooperatively join in the task. *(Romans 12: 8)*
- ◆ **Shepherding**—The pastoral gift of guiding, nurturing, comforting, and protecting a group of believers. *(Ephesians 4: 11; 1 Peter 5: 1-3)*
- ◆ **Mercy**—Cheerful performance of ministry to those who are sick, hurting, or in crisis. *(Romans 12: 8)*
- ◆ **Hospitality**—The desire and talent to graciously share fellowship, food, and lodging in your home. *(1 Peter: 4: 9)*
- ◆ **Giving**—Contributing eagerly and generously to the Lord's work. *(Romans 12: 8)*
- ◆ **Music**—The ability to communicate God's love and one's personal testimony through music. *(1 Corinthians 14: 15, 26)*

It is a common misunderstanding among many evangelical church people that to be charismatic is to speak in tongues. Or, to put it another way, if you do not speak in tongues, you are not a charismatic. But this is not so. If you recognize and use the spiritual gifts within you, whatever they may be, then you are indeed Spirit-filled and may be considered a charismatic.

One who exercises several gifts of the Spirit is not necessarily more spiritual or more Christian than one who uses only one gift. This is the point Paul communicated so forcefully in 1 Corinthians 12 and 13. Pride has no place among those who exercise the Holy Spirit's gifts. Each person's gifts are but tools for ministry, and all gifts are necessary for the body of Christ to function—just as all parts of the human body are necessary for it to function. The issue of tongues should never be held up as a measure of how spiritual one is or whether one is truly a Spirit-filled Christian.

Fruits of the Spirit are attitudes and actions that result from the presence of the Holy Spirit in the Christian's life. In Galatians 5: 22-23, Paul speaks of:

- ◆ Love
- ◆ Joy
- ◆ Peace
- ◆ Patience
- ◆ Kindness
- ◆ Goodness
- ◆ Faithfulness
- ◆ Gentleness
- ◆ Self-control

For purposes of remembering the distinction between Spiritual Gifts and Fruits of the Spirit, we can say that Gifts refer to the tasks performed in serving the Lord, whereas Fruits refer to the loving attitude and ethical actions shown by the servant. We tend to think of someone exercising dramatic gifts as being "really Christian." However, we can see true Christianity by observing the Fruits of the Spirit—a father lovingly hugging his children, a mother joyously giving of herself in patient nurture, someone sticking by a troubled friend with kind acceptance and love, or one controlling the temptation to sin.

Speaking in Tongues is a form of speaking and/or singing praises to God in the Spirit. It is a devotional prayer to the Lord that circumvents the limiting filters of our mind.

In the one who employs the gift of singing in tongues, the Holy Spirit empowers him or her to sing with one's spirit to God's Spirit for the purpose of praise and to be refreshed spiritually. This form of tongues is between the individual and God and requires no interpretation. Its primary value in equipping one for ministry is in the spiritual refreshment it produces for the one caught up in pure spirit to Spirit worship.

Interpretation of Tongues is only necessary when the direction of communication is reversed and God gives a message for the body of Christ through the one speaking in tongues. This calls for someone to interpret to others what God may be saying. That is, one who is equipped with the gift of interpretation communicates the message from God in a known tongue so the church may be edified.

Can a charismatic person, exercising his spiritual gifts, have a slumbering personal spirit? Would not the releasing of the Holy Spirit's power in one's life tend to awaken the personal spirit?

Not necessarily so! It is almost never that the Holy Spirit, alone, awakens a person's personal spirit. We think this is because ours is an incarnational faith, and Jesus wants the church to be involved in this happening. Person to person, Jesus wants people to love each other to life.

Lord, I want to be fully awakened—set free to be transformed by Your power into the glory of Your likeness. I long for a rich and satisfying relationship with you, and the fulfillment of all that You created me to be.

By your grace, Lord, enable me to forgive those who were unable to nurture me to life. Forgive me for all the ways I have withdrawn from intimacy, and held bitterness and negative expectations in my heart. Forgive me for striving to win love and acceptance without the willingness or ability to hold my heart open to others.

Melt my heart of stone, Lord. Fill me with life and give me strength of spirit to persist in risking to choose life. Enable me to be vulnerable to people through whom You would give me nurture of mind, body, soul and spirit.

Set me free from slumber and empower me to bring life and joy to others.

Life Applications:
Sleepwalking in the Spirit

1. In your own words, write a brief definition of each of these terms:

   ♦ Personal Spirit

   ♦ Soul

   ♦ Mind

   ♦ Body

   To reinforce your understanding, explain each of these terms to a friend, or to fellow group members. Discuss your definitions and answer questions, but avoid getting into disputes over disagreement in terms.

2. What is an evangelical Christian? What must happen in the life of an evangelical Christian for one to be considered charismatic?

3. What is a Spiritual Gift? For what purposes are Spiritual Gifts given?

4. Review the list of Spiritual Gifts mentioned on pages 26-28. Which of these are you aware of in your own life? Ask others to reveal to you what gifts they believe you have been given.

5. In your own words, write what is meant by "Fruits of the Spirit."

6. Explain how one might be filled with the Holy Spirit and be exercising Spiritual Gifts, yet not be showing Fruits of the Spirit? If you can, list an example that bothers you in your own life.

7 . Memorize the nine Fruits of the Spirit enumerated in Galatians 5: 22-23. For each, write down a specific way you will attempt to exemplify spiritual fruit in your relationships with others. Keep this list as a daily reminder to be more aware of how your Christian faith can make a difference in your attitude and behavior.

♦ Love

♦ Joy

♦ Peace

♦ Patience

♦ Kindness

♦ Goodness

♦ Faithfulness

♦ Gentleness

♦ Self-Control

Chapter 2
What Causes the Spirit to Slumber?

What causes someone to slumber in the spirit? When we put this question to the Lord in prayer, He revealed to us that when a person slumbers in the spirit it is a result of not yet being fully human.

To understand that, we need to come to a Christian definition of what it means to be human. We are used to dealing with a variety of definitions for "human being" as put forth by the disciplines of anthropology, sociology, psychology, or philosophy. But God has provided a distinctly different definition.

Essentially, to be human is to have an awakened personal spirit by which one identifies and empathizes with others, becomes one with them, and cherishes what is in the other person even more than one's own life.

"Greater love has no one than this, that he lay down his life for his friends." (John 15: 13)

"Each of you should look not only to your own interests, but also to the interests of others." (Philippians 2: 4)

An even shorter way to define being fully human would be to say one word — **Jesus**. Jesus is the one fully human person. God's desire for us is that we are to become more human like Jesus. We are to become *more* human, not less human.

Understanding our humanness

We commonly use the word human in the wrong way. We say: "Oh, I did that wrong thing because of my human nature."

That is absolutely backwards. When we act in hurtful, unethical and immoral ways, it is because we haven't yet developed a fully human nature.

Listen to the word. "Inhumane." We use it commonly in our language but we just don't get the point. What does it mean? We describe someone as being inhumane when that person commits a terrible sin. To be inhumane is to act "not human." If this is the case, why do we say: "I'm guilty of that sin, because after all, I'm only human." WRONG! Absolutely backward. To behave sinfully is to behave in ways that are less than fully human.

We are not talking about humanism here. Humanism is the glorification of the human position — putting man at the center of his universe. Humanism is Satan's copy of what God is doing to transform men and women into the character of Jesus Christ through His saving grace. The goal of *true humanity* is to become more like Jesus. He was the one sent by our Heavenly Father to show us what it is to be fully human.

Ours is an incarnational faith. The scripture tells us *"the Word became flesh" (John 1: 14)*. The Word didn't just visit in flesh, it BECAME flesh. We do not have bodies in which our spirits slosh around like water in a glass, from which one day the spirit will go back to heaven. Each of us is one being, spirit and body flowing together. Through the spirit (the life force) breathed into us by God, we are to become human beings.

The human animal is the only animal which will not become its own kind if not raised by its own kind. You can raise a cow with horses, and it won't get confused and try to whinny. It will still moo and give milk. You can raise a dog with cats, and it won't get confused. It will still bark and raise its leg. A fish is hatched and doesn't need its father and mother. In fact, it often has to flee from its father to avoid being eaten.

But we human animals don't become human just by being born. We don't become human by just existing. We have to be nurtured into becoming human. The human animal is dependent upon its mother and father longer than any species in all of creation. We are not societal by accident; it is by necessity.

The need for affection

There are certain kinds of nurture needed for us to grow in our humanness. The first of these is affection. We do not become human beings unless we experience affectionate touch — as babies, as toddlers, as children growing up, as teenagers, as adults. We do not retain our humanity without continuing to touch others with clean, wholesome love and affection.

Touch imparts life and energy. Touch imparts security and strength. Touch communicates the vital element of meeting spirit to spirit with another person. We have to be held to properly develop our true humanity.

Here is the news for you — the crucial part of the lesson that much of the world has yet to discover. It is extremely difficult to become human beings with fully awakened personal spirits without nurture in the context of the family — from father and mother, grandparents, siblings and other relatives. Fathers are extremely important in this process. They are primary in the awakening of the personal spirits of infants and children. This is not to denigrate mothers, or to undervalue their importance in giving love and care and all kinds of nurture to the child. But fathers were created to fulfill a special role. They have a developmental task to call their children into life as functioning spirits.

> *"And ye fathers, provoke not your children to wrath: but bring them up in the nurture and admonition of the Lord."*
> *(Ephesians 6: 4) (KJV)*

When the baby is conceived, the child needs the father's spirit about the mother; needs to feel the father's presence even while in the womb. The newborn baby needs to be held by the father, to be comforted in the night, to be burped, to be given dry diapers, and to be sung lullabies. This role of the father is important. A newborn baby is familiar with its mother's womb. But outside the womb the baby learns for the first time how to meet another person through the personal spirit. The baby is drawn forth and taught how to function by the father's nurture.

Ideally, the father should be the first person who is primary to the child outside of the womb to give nurture through affectionate touch. This is a different kind of strength than from the mother. The baby's personal spirit flows out into the father and drinks from the father's spirit. The baby blesses the father and the father returns the blessing through loving presence and touch. The baby learns in the spirit how to meet a person other than its mother. The importance of this cannot be over-emphasized.

Listen to the scriptures. The prophet Malachi describes the great day of the coming of the Lord Almighty, when the people must respond to the laws of God or suffer the consequences:

> *"See, I will send you the prophet Elijah before that great and dreadful day of the Lord comes. He will turn the hearts of the fathers to their children, and the hearts of the children to their fathers; or else I will come and strike the land with a curse." (Malachi 4: 5-6)*

The Hebrew culture of the Old Testament was a tribal, patriarchal society in which the father was clearly identified as the head of the family. That role and its subsequent expectations were clearly understood. Malachi might well have said that the hearts of parents must turn to their children and the children to their parents. Or he might well have said that families should be families and their members should take care to nurture one another.

But the message is clear that the father is expected to assume the leadership role in family nurturing. In the purpose of God, fathers are primary in teaching their children's personal spirits how to function.

The need for discipline

The father's responsibility also is to provide the child with admonishment and discipline. Fathers should define limits to their children in respect to how they relate to others in their personal spirits. Fathers should take seriously the task of being strong and firm when needed; to say to the child: "This is where you stop. I am not letting you run amok."

> *"Folly is bound up in the heart of a child, but the rod of discipline will drive it far from him." (Proverbs 22: 15)*

Strong, thoughtful, and loving leadership on the part of the father can create a family environment in which authority is respected, boundaries are understood, communication remains open, and parents can work together to provide discipline the child needs to thrive in the spirit. If the father is not there to provide that very important leadership and personal involvement, a part of the child's spirit withers and falls asleep. This inevitably results in a stunting of emotional and spiritual growth.

The need for strong family structures

Let's consider historically and culturally what is happening in our nation. In Malachi 4:5-6, the prophet spoke of the need for the hearts of fathers to turn to their children, and the hearts of the children to their fathers *"or else I will come and strike the land with a curse."*

That curse is unfolding for us right now. We are living out the consequences of not following the admonition of God for fathers to assume proper family leadership, and for family members to turn to each other in the process of nurturing their personal spirits.

Before the First World War, the nuclear family (father, mother and children) were not isolated from others. Most people lived in the context of an extended family — grandparents, aunts, uncles, and cousins. Society was much less mobile. People tended to live for longer periods of time in geographical proximity to those they grew up with, and they tended to spend more time together and knew each other more intimately.

It was also a more affectionate age, even in the way people expressed themselves. Have you ever read letters written during that period of history? We would think of them today as almost corny. "O my dear soul, without you the sun does not rise, I do not see the moon. You are my very life . . ." It was a mushy, but affectionate age.

During the First World War, when fathers went overseas and were gone for long periods of time, there was still an extended family left behind to fill in the role of the father for young children. There were grandfathers and uncles who spent time with the children, held them affectionately and nurtured them. Consequently, more people grew up having an awakened personal spirit and a heightened sense of true conscience. They were more capable of sustaining relationships, and families tended to stay together.

But after the war, the entire nation became more mobile. Mass production of inexpensive automobiles enabled more people to have better transportation. Families were able to travel greater distances and members of the extended family lived farther apart than was previously practical. Increased industrialization brought more people to the cities from rural areas.

The crash of the stock market and the great depression that followed also tended to disintegrate many families and create even greater mobility. Hundreds of thousands of people migrated to other parts of the nation, seeking better employment opportunities.

Then came World War II. Fathers again went off to war, mothers went to work in war plants, and children grew up in child care centers or in the care of friends. It was not an uncommon experience for men to be away two or three years and come home to toddlers who had never known them. An entire generation of young children missed out on the essential kind of fatherly nurturing they needed in the earliest years to provide them with fully awakened personal spirits.

The Korean War soon followed. And not too many years later, the Vietnam War. Hundreds of thousands of men again were away from their homes and their young children.

When troops came back from all of these wars, they found themselves so psychologically wounded and so far behind in their education and careers, that in many cases they just got their wives pregnant and went off to bury themselves in school or the workforce. Mothers were left to raise the kids. Or, mothers also went to work or school and grandparents or childcare centers were left to raise the kids.

Another entire generation of children made do without close relationships with their dads and/or other primary persons in their lives. The result has been a failure to get the nurturing needed to sustain an awakened personal spirit.

The consequences we are seeing today are reflected in divorce rates. More than half of all marriages fail. Why?

♦ Communication on a deep personal level does not happen when one's spirit is slumbering.

♦ Long-term personal relationships cannot be sustained when one's spirit is slumbering.

♦ A true conscience cannot actively work in one's life to avoid trouble when the personal spirit is slumbering.

♦ Past experiences cannot wisely be remembered to prevent future mistakes when one's spirit is slumbering.

♦ A close relationship with God which will heal woundedness cannot be developed when one's spirit is slumbering.

Do you understand what is happening? Families are disintegrating and generations of people with slumbering spirits are raising ensuing generations of slumbering spirits. The result is the curse of entire communities trying to live without adequate communication skills, without loving interpersonal relationships, without true conscience, without respect for others and the logic of law and order.

Marian Wright Edelman in her award-winning book, *The Measure of Our Success*, expresses her belief that the greatest threat to our nation's security and future does not come from external enemies, but from the enemy within — specifically "our loss of strong, moral family and community values and support."

She confesses that, like so many parents, she worries about spending too much time and energy providing her children with opportunities and "things" that she didn't have growing up, and shielding them from problems and barriers she faced as a black child and woman. She feels it is most important to clearly share the positive experiences she did have while growing up — family, community, and spiritual values that helped immunize her against the plagues of indifference, defeatism, negativism, selfishness, and hopelessness.

Our nation is experiencing a crisis in moral values because moral values should be a part of the nurture and teaching in every home, but are not. For the first time in our nation's history, many communities cannot build a school without making it look like a prison. Schools have to be surrounded by fences, with limited access, guarded doors, and metal detectors. This is to keep students in for their own protection and to keep drug dealers out who with no conscience would prey on students. Or, to keep out the vandals who would come in and with no conscience rip up the classrooms. Specially trained guards have to patrol the school hallways to keep students from fighting, or to confiscate guns and knives from those who do not know how to communicate except through threats and violence.

Because so many people have no respect for others and no conscience about wrongdoing, even times of celebration can break into drunken violence. This happened following the

the Chicago Bulls' basketball team winning three consecutive NBA titles, and in Dallas after the Cowboy's 1993 Super Bowl football victory.

Deprivation of nurture

Why do we have this state of affairs? Because entire segments of our society have been so deprived of nurture in the home, and have had little or no spiritual influence from their families — particularly from fathers. Consequently, their personal spirits are virtually dead.

A few years ago, we were speaking at an Episcopal church in the heart of Brooklyn, New York. As we were about to go out for lunch, the rector warned us that it was a very rough neighborhood, and that we should stay in groups for our own safety. He made it clear that we should *never* go on the street alone at night. He said that if we had to be out alone at any time and saw a gang of young people approaching, that we should not walk, but run for safety! Otherwise, he said, they will beat you, rob you, and may kill you and walk away laughing. He told us they have had no fathers to nurture them. They have no conscience, and no concern over doing harm to other people.

This condition is not limited to the streets of New York, Detroit, Chicago or Los Angeles. Even in the prosperous suburbs of less notorious cities, it is not uncommon to find adolescent gangs, random vandalism, and widespread drug use. A major contributing factor to these kinds of problems is that more than half of the children come from homes headed by single parents, or from second-or third-marriage homes with children who are "his, hers, and ours," with no clear sense of close-knit family unity.

Even children who have been nurtured with loving care in the stability of a strong home are not without the danger of slipping into spiritual slumber as adults. We live in a secular society and it is easy to slide into patterns of superficiality and non-involvement. We anesthetize the spirit through:

- Impersonality in the workplace and in the neighborhood.

- Isolation from the natural extended family through distance or divorce.

- Little or no involvement in personal devotions or in corporate worship through the church.

- Busy work and recreational schedules that allow little time for relationship building and intimate conversation.

- Casual attitudes toward sexual involvement outside of marriage.

- Overexposure to violence, resulting in insensitivity to the hurts and feelings of others.

Are you beginning to comprehend? Do you understand why there is so little concern for the rights and welfare of others, so much fragmentation in the family, so much divorce, so much crime? The curse spoken of in Malachi 4: 5-6 is of our own making.

We are reaping the consequences of a poverty of nurture that has crippled the personal spirits of growing children.

The essential structures of love and discipline from parents and the extended family have not been intact — and consequently are not intact today.

Even more specifically, fathers are not being fathers. When fathers do not nurture their children with affectionate touching and the steady hand of love and discipline, the personal spirits of the children are stunted. What kind of world will we have if the continuing trend of spiritual slumber goes unchanged? We need only to look at Scripture to see a very clear catalog of qualities that will dominate our society. (Or is that time already here?)

*"People will be lovers of themselves, lovers of money, boast-
ful, proud, abusive, disobedient to their parents, ungrateful,
unholy, without love, unforgiving, slanderous, without self-
control, brutal, not lovers of the good, treacherous, rash,
conceited, lovers of pleasure rather than lovers of God—
having a form of godliness but denying its power."
(2 Timothy 3: 2-4)*

Saint Paul is not speaking here of the world at large. He is
speaking of those who are in the church—who "have a form of
godliness" but deny its power. We cannot escape the curse of
slumbering spirits just by being actively involved in the church.
People with slumbering spirits can accept the plan of salvation
mentally and be born anew, yet relate only to law, theology, and
doctrine rather than the person of Jesus. They don't meet Jesus
on a personal level because their spirits are asleep.

People can get into a charismatic church and be caught up in
the emotional excitement of raising their hands in praise and
singing. But all too often if the Lord left the worship service,
they wouldn't know the difference because they are only into the
worship form. They don't know Jesus because their spirits are
slumbering.

Others can get into a liturgical church and be emotionally
moved by the rituals and symbols of the service (again, the worship form). But they don't know God because their spirits are
asleep.

The slumbering spirit is the crux of what is wrong with
many people today and the primary key of what has happened to
infect the Church with apathy. Slumbering spirits have brought
on a crisis of conscience and a growing epidemic of callousness
and immorality. We must understand the nature of slumbering
spirits if we are to understand why there is so little communication between people and so many broken relationships. We face
major problems that all boil down to the need for the hearts of
fathers and mothers to turn to their children and to provide the

kind of involved, loving, touching, and disciplined nurture that is essential to keep the personal spirit alive and vitally awake.

Looking past problems with hopeful hearts!

You may be wondering right now, "Well, good grief, my father and/or mother never provided the kind of close and loving nurture described here. So is there any hope for me?"

In thinking about this, don't panic or go into depression. What you will be doing is ending your loneliness. You no longer will have to think that you are the only hypocrite in the church. Many others share in your condition. As you become aware of the ways in which your spirit slumbers, you can begin to focus on how to overcome that prior lack of nurture.

As you read on in the next three chapters, you will have opportunity to consider ten primary characteristics of an awakened spirit and the common characteristics of persons whose spirits are slumbering. As you evaluate yourself, you probably will discover that your spirit is slumbering in several areas.

Because we are all in the same soup, we can also be in the same blessing. If you understand where you seem to be most asleep in your spirit, you can be more aware of how to compensate for that and how to seek healing through God's power and the love of Christian friends.

As we come together,
we can begin to love each other
back to life.

❧   **H**eavenly Father, give me an understanding of what it means to be truly human — to walk each day in the steps of the Lord Jesus Christ who is the model of love, goodness, and grace that You have set out as our guide.

Help me to live happily under the discipline of Your grace, and in turn to discipline those entrusted to my charge with the steady hand of Your wisdom and unconditional love.

Help me to both give and receive affection with humility and purity of heart.

Help me to build strong and nurturing family structures, undergirded with reliance on You, my loving Heavenly Father.

Help me to fix my sight on the Lord Jesus who is that clear point of light with which You penetrate the wilderness of evil that surrounds us. Give me the strength and courage always to set my course straight for the light of my Savior's grace and restoring love.

Life Applications:
What Causes the Spirit to Slumber

1. Review what is written in this chapter about the way we use the words *human* and *inhumane*. What concept of human nature were you taught as a child? Have you grown up understanding humanness to be a high ideal, or a natural state of sin to be overcome?

2. Based on what you have learned in this chapter, write a new definition in your own words of what it means to be fully human.

3. This chapter lists three needs which must be fulfilled in order for one to maintain an awakened personal spirit: **affection, loving discipline**, and **strong family structures.** What is your personal story of how well these needs were met as you were growing up? (Share with a friend the feelings you hold about each of these needs. Pray together about your feelings.)

4. Read 2 Timothy 3: 2-4. List ways in which Paul's description of those Christians might be a mirror of developing characteristics in your own life?

5. If you could go back in time and create an environment in which to be re-nurtured in a more positive way, what would that experience be like? Share your description with a friend, or in your small group. Ask the friend or small group to be a vessel through which God can supply nurture to you now.

6. If you believe you are in need of re-nurturing at this point in your life in order to wake your slumbering spirit, what sources of help can you think of that would contribute toward fulfilling that need? Make a list.

Chapter 3
Relating to God

In the next three chapters we will explore ten ways an awakened personal spirit equips us to function in our full humanity. We will also illustrate what happens when our spirits slumber in these areas.

When considering these ten characteristics of an awakened personal spirit, be aware that no one is entirely asleep or awake. Each person possesses his or her own distinctive spiritual make-up. Some will be more asleep than others. Some may have areas in their life in which they are fully awake while they are woefully asleep in other areas. Some people may slip in and out of sleepiness, being alert at times and then drifting off into insensitivity.

As diagnostic tools in counseling sessions, we ask a series of questions to determine if a person's spirit is slumbering. Each of the ten sections dealing with characteristics of an awakened personal spirit will begin with a diagnostic question. Consider these carefully to help you get in touch with functions of your personal spirit most in need of awakening.

The first four characteristics of an awakened personal spirit have to do with one's ability to relate to God.

Feeling God's presence
in corporate worship

When you are in a worship service and others are joy-ously caught up in the preaching of the Word, singing, and praise, can you really feel God's presence, or do you just have to know by faith that He is there?

When God moves upon us in worship, He does not move upon our minds or hearts first, but upon our personal spirits.

"Yet a time is coming and has now come when the true wor-shipers will worship the Father in spirit and in truth, for they are the kind of worshipers the Father seeks. God is spirit, and His worshipers must worship in spirit and in truth." (John 4: 23-24)

God quickens our spirits and enables us to worship. Listen to the "Magnificat" (the song of Mary). The King James transla-tion helps us by its use of the tenses in which Mary spoke:

*"My soul **doth** magnify the Lord and my spirit **hath** rejoiced in God my Savior." (Luke 1: 46-47)*

Because Mary's spirit **had** rejoiced in God, she was quick-ened (caused to be enlivened or to be more sensitive and aware). This enabled the power of her spirit to flow out **presently** through her mind, character, and personality to magnify and worship the Lord.

A person who has an awakened personal spirit can come into a group which is worshiping and feel the presence of God's Holy Spirit flowing into the worshipers. This experience is appre-hended differently by different persons, of course, depending upon the form of worship that is most uplifting to the individual.

It may come in the wonder of participation in mass at a cathedral, in the singing of hymns in a country church, or in the prayers and praise of a close home fellowship of friends. The common element of the corporate worship experience is the feeling of being caught up into the presence of God. We praise God and sing to God, aided by the Holy Spirit. Worship happens when God comes and meets us and catches us up to Himself.

People who have slumbering spirits have difficulty getting from praise to worship because they are unable to experience the exhilarating feeling that should result when God's Spirit comes on them.

Most of the time they will say: "I believe God is aware of our worship, but I have never really felt His presence in the way you are describing."

Such persons may sometimes feel God's presence as a flicker for a moment, but they are unable to stay and rest in His presence. Their personal spirit does not enable them to let go emotionally and enter fully into corporate worship. The result may be a wandering mind, visual distractions, inability to be comfortable with unfamiliar worship forms, preoccupation with one's problems, or even distrust or skepticism about fellow worshipers.

For whatever reason, God's abiding presence is not a reality because the person's spirit is not alive enough to let the glory of praise and worship overcome the barriers the self erects. The spirit is numbed by slumber and true worship in the presence of God seldom if ever happens.

Feeling God's presence in private devotions

> *During times of prayer and private devotions, do you have a strong sense of God's presence and power lifting you up in real worship?*

A person having a fully awakened personal spirit will be able to individually and privately pray, read Scripture and praise God with a real sense of the presence of the Lord Jesus Christ. This will be accompanied by feeling His glory all around, lifting you up, refreshing you, and equipping you for the day.

> *"But it is the spirit in a man, the breath of the Almighty, that gives him understanding." (Job 32: 8)*

This sense of spiritual presence does not happen when our personal spirit is slumbering. When asked about feeling God's presence in private devotions, a slumberer's characteristic reply might be: "No, I can't, but at least I can spend time in Bible study, and I make that a part of my devotions."

When our spirit is slumbering, even Bible study becomes an exercise in reading mere words. Have you ever had the experience of reading a book when you are distracted or your mind is wandering onto other things? Suddenly you realize you have read an entire paragraph without comprehending what you just read.

That is a common experience for those who attempt to have personal devotions when their spirit is slumbering. The focus and feeling of Bible reading are lost. The words have no life because you cannot receive the quickening breath of God to sensitize your understanding.

You cannot maintain an attitude of sustained prayer because of a wandering mind or inability to be open to communication with God. You run dry and the experience falls dead. When this happens, it is easy to give up trying to have a personal devotional time.

Personal devotions require ability to enjoy being alone, to be quiet, to focus on prayer and inspirational thoughts, to read scripture, to praise, and to quietly listen to God's voice. These are characteristics of the personal spirit that God is able to quicken into devotional sensitivity.

Do you find it uncomfortable to be alone, preferring always to have someone with you, to go shopping, to travel, to study, even to be entertained? Do you find it uncomfortable to experience silence, always wanting to have a radio or TV playing, or to be engaged in some kind of busy activity or conversation? Some might protest that being alone or experiencing quiet moments is boring to them. But for the person with an awakened personal spirit, times alone or times of quiet solitude characteristically are stimulating and exciting times because the spirit can then soar unimpeded by distractions or the demands of other people. It is in this environment that focused devotion can result in very rewarding times of worship and intimacy with the Lord.

Of course, personality types vary greatly. Some people are more introverted by nature and seem to draw energy and affirmation from within themselves. They tend to be more comfortable working alone or spending time by themselves. Other people have more extraverted personalities and draw their energy from outside themselves, getting stimulation, companionship, and affirmation in the presence of others.

However, in our experience of dealing with many different people with different personality types, those who have awakened personal spirits are growing toward more security in their inner being and can relax and focus during time spent alone. Even the extravert can enjoy the silence. The spirit is able to let go and be aware of God's presence. The senses are heightened and true worship becomes a reality.

Experiencing real communication with God

Do you ever hear the voice of God? Do you ever have spiritual dreams or visions, or know in some other way with certainty what God is saying to you ?

Be honest now. Are you among the skeptics? When you hear someone say he hears the voice of God, is your first reaction that he is either a psychotic or a religious charlatan? Unfortunately, that is the common reaction for most people in society today because listening to God is such an uncommon practice.

Indeed, there are insane people who think they hear God but actually do not. There are dishonest religious manipulators who make questionable claims on what God asks of us in order to attract followers and make financial gain. And there are religious cult leaders who have disgraced the Christian church with wildly distorted teachings and ridiculous claims of messages from God that only serve their own perverse purposes. But there also is the reality of God directly communicating with those whose spirits are awake enough to hear Him. God guides and enriches those who listen to Him in spirit and in truth.

A major part of hearing what is said to you is a result of paying attention. Particularly in our age of multi-media and multi-tasking (doing more than one thing at the same time), it is difficult to stay tuned in enough to hear even the audible messages that come our way.

If you have an active child involved in a distracting game, it is often necessary as a parent to get his attention by gently taking his face in your hands and saying firmly, "Now look at me and pay attention to what I'm saying!" Sometimes it is helpful to ask that the message be repeated verbally, to be certain it was properly understood.

God will seldom grab us by the face and make us listen, although sometimes a crisis in life may serve that purpose. Generally, listening to God takes practice. You have to try to pay attention, and you have to be aware of some of the subtle ways God communicates His will.

Ability to hear God communicate is heightened by an awakened spirit. If one is not aware that God is attempting to communicate directly, it may be that the spirit to whom God is speaking is too numbed by sleep for the message to penetrate the mind.

The typical reply to our question is: "No, I guess I've got to believe that those people who keep saying the Lord tells them things are not fooling themselves, but God never talks to me."

Another typical reply might be, "I believe God answers prayers, but I don't think He speaks directly to people in ways they can actually hear."

People who have an awakened personal spirit know God often speaks through dreams, and they stand ready to listen. They may have dreams that come true, or that have distinct symbolic meanings that hold a message from God they can clearly understand. They also get pictures or visions in their minds which communicate a message. Sometimes they may even hear the voice of God speaking to their mind, as it were, or even audibly. God speaks from His Spirit to our spirit. But a spirit that is asleep cannot hear.

"... as it is written, No eye has seen, nor ear has heard, no mind has conceived what God has prepared for those who love him—but God has revealed it to us by His Spirit. The Spirit searches all things, even the deep things of God."
(1 Corinthians 2: 9-10)

Receiving inspiration from God

> *Do you sense that it is God who inspires you with fresh
> ideas and creative ability?*

God wants to give us inspiration. This inspiration is not just
in the Christian context; it is the unleashing of creative insight
and power in all areas of life.

♦ Envisioning creative ideas

♦ Building fresh and exciting new solutions

♦ Interpreting with sensitivity

♦ Simplifying the complex

♦ Clarifying the obscure

♦ Integrating the diverse

♦ Expressing with power

♦ Leading with charisma

Have you ever known someone who has studied poetry and
knows meter, scanning, imagery and all the literary forms; yet,
the poetry that person attempts to write is doggerel? The message
is pedantic, the imagery is flat, and the words have no life or
power. What is lacking is inspiration.

On the other hand, someone else may not even be a serious
student of poetry, yet that person's writing practically jumps off
the page. The poetry has internal rhythm, powerful imagery, and
sensitivity of expression that captures your imagination and
moves you emotionally. It is inspired.

Similarly, a person may study painting and know symmetri-
cal and asymmetrical balance, color theory, and all the other
techniques of visual art. But the paintings they create are me-
chanical. They are nothing but technique and lack feeling. Another painter may apply a few simple brush strokes and you
look at it with wonder. Even in the simplicity, there is power

and something creatively unique. What is the difference? One has inspiration added to his discipline; the other doesn't.

We have an engineer friend who characterizes the co-workers in his office as fitting two basic categories: drones and innovators. Drones are engineers who primarily apply the common solutions that other people have already worked out. Drones seldom get an original idea. Their thinking is very practical but also very flat. They lack inspiration to come up with innovative solutions.

On the other hand, he sees some engineers as being very creative innovators. They get all kinds of ideas and are excited by the challenge of finding new and efficient ways to solve engineering problems. The difference is in their ability to integrate their knowledge, logic and exposure to new ideas into inspired thinking. There is a creative spark which is ignited by an awakened personal spirit.

It must be noted here again that everyone has a personal spirit and God's inspiration can flow to believers and non-believers alike. In fact, religiously neutral persons may be better equipped to receive creative inspiration. Creativity flows more easily when your spirit is open to the possibility of new ideas and you freely risk the dangers of striking out into unexplored territories. Such creativity requires a kind of singular focus for inspiration truly to take root. In this sense, an awakened personal spirit has less to do with religion than with spiritual openness.

Inspiration often comes more readily to the young at heart who can deal with life from a more focused and simple point of view. Thomas Hart Benton, perhaps the most influential American mural painter in this century, was known for the wonderful simplicity of his images portraying the indomitable spirit of man. As an active artist painting well into his eighties, he preferred the company of people under twenty years of age in his studio. According to Benton, only the very young were capable of dealing with the fresh ideas that so stimulated him.

One's Christian belief and commitment may or may not be a factor in how awakened the spirit is to receive gifts from God. This is especially true in the area of creative inspiration. It would be wonderful to experience one's Christian faith enhancing creative capacity as has been the case with many artists, writers, scientists, and world leaders throughout history. However, oftentimes the Christian believer is so locked up in the forms of religion that the spirit is given little chance to soar. Or, one may be so burdened with the responsibilities of family care or of ministry that the spirit is not free enough to recognize inspiration from God, or to fly with it when it comes.

God pours out inspiration to every awakened spirit capable of receiving it. Wonderful harmony can result in a life when God's inspiration flows into the awakened personal spirit of a Spirit-filled Christian. But we must recognize too that God's inspiration flows into the awakened spirits of non-believers as well, and that they often produce wonderfully creative works of art, music, literature and scientific invention.

Lord, I pray that you awaken my spirit to experience awe and wonder at the beauty of Your creation. Kindle Your light inside me so I can see the brightness of color, the flowing grace of a field of ripened wheat, tender affection in the eyes of a loved one.

Open my ears to the music of a child's laughter, the exciting sound of a ball cracking against a bat, the pleasant swish of underbrush as I walk a path on my way to a fishing stream.

Let me be refreshed and lifted by Your presence, comfortable with You even in silence, sensitive to Your direction, comforted by Your Spirit.

And Lord, make me a vessel to catch Your good gifts of inspiration with excitement, that I might share them with holy and considerate zeal.

Life Applications:
Relating to God

1 . Review the four characteristics of an awakened personal spirit listed in this chapter. Rate yourself on a scale of one to five (1= least awake, 5= most awake) by circling the degree to which you feel your spirit is in an awakened state in each characteristic.

Feel God's presence in corporate worship.
    1 2 3 4 5

Feel God's presence in private devotion.
    1 2 3 4 5

Aware of God communicating with you.
    1 2 3 4 5

Receive inspiration from God.
    1 2 3 4 5

2. In corporate worship, what limits your fully experiencing God's presence? Can you identify what it is that distracts you? On a sheet of paper draw a line down the middle from top to bottom. On the left side make a list of things that commonly distract you during worship. On the right, jot down ways in which you might lessen those distractions to become more focused on personally relating to God.

3. In private devotions, try these simple exercises to encourage more frequent and more focused devotional life:
   ♦ Pray flash prayers frequently throughout the day. Make them simple, eyes-open, conversations with God to ask for help, for His uplifting presence, or to thank and praise Him. Try to develop a running attitude of prayer.

◆ To shut out visual distractions during your time of private devotions, light a candle in a darkened and quiet room and focus your attention on the flame to help you concentrate on the presence of God's Holy Spirit. Pray aloud to God about whatever comes to mind. Be honest and confessional without trying to be eloquent.

◆ Listen to gospel music on tape with ear phones. Darken the room or close your eyes to shut out distractions. Listen carefully to the meaning of the words. If you prefer, listen to classical music. Imagine your entire body being bathed in the presence of the Holy Spirit.

4. To enhance deeper communication between you and God, begin by accepting in faith that it can and will happen if you allow yourself to be open enough. Create an environment in which you can pay close attention to the ways God might be speaking to you.

◆ Read the Beatitudes from the 5th chapter of Matthew by candlelight. Do not read just to get finished. Pause with each verse and ponder its meaning. Pray that God might reveal a special message to you from each passage. Take time to listen for an answer. God may speak through your own thoughts, especially if they come into consciousness easily and restfully.

◆ Sit on the beach and watch the waves come in, or go into the woods and quietly observe nature all around you. Think carefully about what you are experiencing. Is God unfolding symbolic messages to you as you experience the wonders of nature?

◆ Do you have recurring dreams? Keep a pad and pen by your bed. As soon as you wake up, think back through your dream and then jot down what you dreamed before you forget. Discuss your dreams with a Christian friend, and consider ways God may be communicating

with you through them. Dreams are usually more symbolic than literal. Look for the messages within the
symbols.

5. Pray for God's inspiration that you might become a more
   creative and innovative person. Ask Him to help you see ordinary things in new and creative ways. Pay attention when
   you get a fresh idea. Say "Thank you, God!" Then use the
   idea by sharing it with others. Build on your new discoveries
   with a grateful heart.

Chapter 4
Relating to Others

Transcending time

Do lessons of the past grip you with sufficient power to keep you from making the same mistakes again? Or do your memories fade? Do future possibilities excite you enough to energize sticking it out through problems, and help you make good decisions? Or do you feel stuck in the present moment?

The ability to learn from the past and to project into the future is what we call "transcending time." It is the ability to connect what was, what is, and what can be.

For example: a couple comes in to see us for counseling. They have awakened personal spirits, but they have some trouble spots in their marriage that will require hard work from both of them to smooth out. Because their spirits are awake, they have the ability to remember good things in their marriage. They can also project into the future that once they get past their present trouble, their relationship will be glorious again. Their spirits enable them to connect what was, what is, and what can be with power to affect their emotions and create hope. They can make sense of the cause and effect relationships required to get them from where they are to where they want to go.

On the other hand, another couple comes in for counseling but they have no ability to remember the good things of the past with any compelling sense of reality. They have no ability to project into the future to believe that a good relationship can be restored. They are trapped in the present. They can't transcend the present moment and can only focus on their current hurts, quarrels and unhappiness. Their slumbering spirits have made them dysfunctional and ill-equipped to salvage their relationship and their marriage.

The young man mentioned previously who had trouble paying his bills, also had a slumbering spirit which kept him from transcending time. He could focus only on the present moment. When he saw something he liked, he would buy it right then in his excitement. If he didn't have the money, he would charge it with no thought to how he would have to pay for it later. By the time the creditors began calling, his memory of the purchase was so far removed that it had no reality to him. He saw the bill collectors only as a nuisance invading his present moment.

Have you ever been to a church service and experienced a powerful sermon in which the pastor warned, as Saint Paul did, that we will all be accountable for our deeds before the Lord? When someone goes out after hearing such a sermon and sins as though no judgment day is coming, you wonder: "How could he do that?"

Why? Because preaching to a person with a slumbering spirit about the judgment day coming is like putting a quarter into a broken vending machine. It falls through to reject; there is no place to catch the message. His spirit is slumbering. The future and the past have no compelling reality to him because he focuses only on the present moment.

Communicating with others on a deep personal level

In conversations, do you often sense or feel what the other person is feeling, so that you understand the meaning even before the words have been fully spoken? Or, do you just have to figure out with your mind what others are trying to say?

It is a wonderfully refreshing feeling to be in conversation with someone when your spirits just seem to latch on to each other. When that happens you become so tuned in to each other that you can leap-frog your thoughts. You don't even have to finish a sentence before the other person understands your meaning. You not only hear the words, but you correctly sense the intent and the feeling of the conversation. That kind of communication is exciting and very fulfilling.

On the other hand, have you ever been in conversation with someone, thinking he or she was tracking with you, when unexpectedly the person says something that comes clear out of left field? You think: "Where did that come from? I thought we were tuned in to each other."

When this happens, it probably means that your conversational partner was following you with his mind rather than with his spirit. In order to communicate with you, he had to figure out with his mind how to respond. When the conversation took a curve, the mind couldn't follow. He just lost his focus and missed you altogether.

Good communication is essential for the intimacy level that should exist between close personal friends, within family groups, and between husband and wife. The kind of communication we are referring to here is much more than the ability to make conversation. Interesting talk can happen without revealing yourself on a personal feeling level.

When a man and woman commit themselves in a bond of marriage, there should be a developing intimacy level in which they can really come to understand and to know each other from their hearts. Spirit to spirit communication between persons results in being able to read each other's facial expressions or eyes, and to be able to sense emotional states without words being spoken. It results in appropriateness of response and behavior so that you do not violate the other person's feelings with impulsiveness or misunderstandings. This kind of intimate communication can develop in various ways; through self-revealing talk, shared experiences, body language, sexual union, and the subtle communications of the spirit.

Building intimate relationships requires presence, and quality of presence is measured in terms of the self revelation of meeting each other spirit to spirit. If the spirit is dysfunctional in a slumbering state, then communication on a deep personal level cannot happen.

To evaluate your own awareness of how awake your spirit is in this area, consider these questions:

- ◆ Do you have several close personal friends you share with deeply and regularly?

- ◆ When you talk with a person, can you comfortably maintain eye contact during your conversation?

- ◆ How comfortable are you in sharing with your friends the most personal things about your life?

- ◆ How well do you think you know your spouse? Are you able to express feelings clearly, or do you frequently miscommunicate or choose not to really communicate at all?

- ◆ Ask your mate to share with you how sensitive you are in understanding his or her needs, motives, responses, and heart-felt concerns.

Sustaining long-term personal relationships

Do you have a number of close relationships, which through good times and bad, have remained strong over a period of many years?

Family structures have become so fragmented and our concept of who we are so confused, that we are producing more and more slumbering spirits with each generation. When two people with slumbering spirits marry and have children, their children are likely to be asleep in their spirits as well, so we wind up having generation after generation of families who develop serious dysfunctions.

Inability to communicate adequately is a major cause of problems among family members. When two people with slumbering spirits get together, it is very difficult for them to tune in to each other. When they talk, it is as though an invisible wall surrounds them, preventing real hearing so that they miss one another. Consequently, they remain isolated and alone, confined to superficial chatter. Their conversation is limited to the surface meaning of each other's words, and they miss the real feeling and intention behind what is being said. Their spirits do not meet and they can't sense what the other person wants and needs. This results in inappropriate responses which subsequently make each partner feel isolated and lonely.

Such persons wind up being tremendously lonely. They can't hear the spirits of others and they haven't learned to really communicate from their own spirits. They just shadow box about issues, reaching out only with their minds to grasp others. It is no wonder that with such poor communication, relationships soon break down. When the spirit slumbers and communication is so difficult, frustration and loneliness set in. A couple may live together, yet remain in spiritual isolation in a dying relationship.

Long term friendships and marriages are built between people who can engage each other's spirits, who can listen and talk on deep and intimate levels. Relationships are sustained by people who can talk out their differences, flex and bend, and grow stronger together because of what they have shared. Communication that builds and sustains relationships is one of the most important functions of the personal spirit.

For the Christian counselor, such communication is the most important function. The counselor must be able to tune in and feel with the other person, so that what is said is appropriate to the needs of the client. If you cease to be appropriate, you violate the process with any insight you may have because you say it at the wrong time, at the wrong place, and in the wrong way. Your spirit must be awake enough to really listen, and it must be open enough to care about what is being said and aware of what is not being said.

Experiencing the glory of Christian marital sex

Do you experience sexual relations in your marriage as deeply fulfilling, intimate, and spiritual experiences that cause you to cherish only your spouse as a sexual partner?

If you are not already aware of this, we want to confirm to you that there is a special glory to Christian marital sex. The glory depends on the Holy Spirit singing through the wife's spirit, through every cell of her body, into the husband to tell him who he is. The glory also depends on the Holy Spirit singing through the husband's spirit, through every cell of his body, into the wife to bless and fulfill her.

We want you to hear this as carefully as it can be said. There can never be glory of this kind in sex outside of marriage. It is an absolute impossibility. It doesn't matter how much the man thinks he is in love with the woman and she with him, or how well they communicate. It absolutely cannot be because the Holy Spirit will not sing in immoral places. We need to get that clear.

A man may say he has had better sex with a woman other than his wife. Of course that may be true if he and his sex partner have been opening their hearts to one another, and he hasn't been doing that with his wife. But good sex and the glory of sex are altogether different. The glory does not come except through the Holy Spirit singing through the husband and wife to each other, and this is an experience that only comes with awakened personal spirits. Take a good look at the fifth chapter of Proverbs:

"Drink water from your own cistern,
And fresh water from your own well.
Should your springs be dispersed abroad,

streams of water in the streets?
Let them be yours alone,
And not for strangers with you.
Let your fountain be blessed,
And rejoice in the wife of your youth.
As a loving hind and a graceful doe,
Let her breasts satisfy you at all times,
Be exhilarated always with her love.
For why should you, my son,
be exhilarated by an adulteress?
And embrace the bosom of a foreigner?"
(Proverbs 5: 15-20) (NAS)

Husbands, your wife is the fountain God has given you. She is your drink of water. Her spirit is there to refresh you. Women have what our son Loren loves to call "chest power." It doesn't depend on the size of the breasts. It depends on the flow of the spirit. Power to refresh flows from the woman's breasts.

As a pastor and counselor, sometimes I (John) come home from ministering to other people feeling completely exhausted. Even more than exhausted, it feels as though I have poured myself out until there is not a drop of humanity left in me. I lose the capability to be human with the kids. I feel like I am just dying inside. I need to be touched. In such a state, if my wife Paula comes at me with a lot of talk, she will miss me. But if she warmly embraces me, I can feel her spirit flowing into me. This lines me up again, tells me who I am, and refills me with joy and vivacity.

Of course, the Holy Spirit of God is the first source of refreshment, but the Holy Spirit decides most often to refresh humanly through our spouses. That's the way He wants to do it. This is a way of saying to you women, when your husband comes home, don't come at him with a lot of talking. Give him a big hug and hold on. You just let him think that you need it, but he needs it as much or more than you do.

To be earthy and practical here as well, we always say to young couples in marriage that pajamas are a great thing to hang on the bed posts in case of fire. Clothes insulate the flow of the electricity of your personal spirit.

Our counsel to married couples is to spend quiet time lying close together. Let your spirits sing into each other and bring refreshment. If you really experience the glory of Christian marital sex, you'll find that it is so good, so clean, so holy, so exhilarating that it will take your breath away. That kind of glory is the best deterrent to immorality. The Scripture speaks clearly to the foolishness of adultery.

But a man who commits adultery lacks judgment; whoever does so destroys himself." (Proverbs 6: 32)

For out of the heart come evil thoughts, murder, adultery, sexual immorality, theft, false testimony, slander."
(Matthew 15: 19)

"Flee from sexual immorality. All other sins a man commits are outside his body, but he who sins sexually sins against his own body. Do you not know that your body is the temple of the Holy Spirit, who is in you, whom you have received from God?" (1 Corinthians 6: 18-19)

To commit adultery is to cause your sexual partner to tell you a lie about yourself. It confuses the issue of who you are and who you belong to. Saint Paul explains in 1 Corinthians 6:15 that the act of joining yourself to a person sexually unites your spirit with that person. When you have been united to more than one person in sexual unions, it fragments your spirit, it divides you against yourself, it betrays the holiness of your marriage relationship, and it defiles the sanctity of your body as the dwelling place of God's Holy Spirit. This is a heavy price to pay to satisfy your lust.

Unfortunately, many people have bought the lie that it does not matter what you do with your body. "After all," they say, "what harm does it do to rub your body against another person as long as it is between two consenting adults?" This is the thinking of an underdeveloped conscience—the insensitive rationalization of a personal spirit who experiences life superficially.

Casual or recreational sex is a sell-out to a lower self. Such a self has not caught the vision of how wonderful a sexual relationship can be, when blessed by God and entered into with a sense of its true holiness. It is difficult for any of us to escape the way our culture seduces us to think of beauty. We get hung up on slender young bodies as the standard of sexuality. When a wife has carried several children and her body is not as shapely as it was before, a husband can easily be drawn to some new and beautiful young thing who wanders into his life. Without an awakened personal spirit to stimulate true conscience, he may act on his impulses and become sexually involved outside marriage. In doing this, he throws away the glory. And the sad part is, he may not even realize that there was a glory to throw away.

> **❧   Lord,** break me out of the tyranny of my immediate problems and desires. Help me to remember past events responsibly, and experience hope for tomorrow. Enable me to meet others, to communicate beyond words, to get in touch with my own feelings and especially the feelings of others.
>
> Teach me the holiness and glory of sexual intimacy. Set me free from fear of vulnerability and the greed of self-gratification. Enable me to cherish and bless my mate with every cell of my being.
>
> Forgive my past sexual sins by which I have wounded God, others, and myself. Separate my spirit from that of every other person with whom I have been intimate. Wash me clean, and enable me to relate wholly and only to my spouse.

Life Applications:
Relating to Others

1. Review the four characteristics of an awakened personal spirit listed in this chapter. Rate yourself on a scale of one to five (1= least awake, 5= most awake) by circling the degree to which you feel your spirit is in an awakened state for each.

    Transcending time.
       1 2 3 4 5

    Communicating with others on a deep level.
       1 2 3 4 5

    Sustaining long-term personal relationships.
       1 2 3 4 5

    Experiencing the glory of Christian marital sex.
       1 2 3 4 5

2. Now, have your spouse or a close friend rate you using the same scale, without having seen your answers.

3. Write down, or discuss with your group, three lessons you have learned from your mistakes in dealing with others which have helped you avoid repeating mistakes in the present.

4. In what areas of your life do you consider yourself to be most vulnerable to making decisions without fully considering the consequences?

Discuss with your group or a friend how you could improve on making more careful and sensible life decisions.

5. Describe your *feelings* about sharing your very personal concerns with others. Is it painful to be self-revealing and vulnerable, or do you find it refreshing? Do you have several friends with whom you regularly share from your heart? What might it take to free you up to be even more intimate in your communication with others?

6. Do you regret having lost touch with a number of people you formerly considered to be close friends? Why did you lose touch? Do you want to rebuild those relationships? If so, write down the names of three people you will call or write this week to get back in touch! Share this commitment with your group or a friend to encourage you and hold you accountable to follow through.

7. How do you *feel* about the role of sex in your life? Is sex for you a glorious and holy experience? What actions or changes in attitude are you willing to take to help restore your sex life to a higher plane of spirituality?

   Discuss the relationship of sex and your spiritual awareness with your spouse or the one you love. Consider whether this is an issue important enough to deal with together in Christian counseling.

8. If you have thrown away the glory and the uniqueness of marital sex by having union with others, before marriage or during marriage, go to someone whose confidentiality you can trust (preferably a pastor or priest) and make confession. (James 5: 16).

   Ask for absolution (pronouncement of forgiveness) as in John 20: 23.

   Ask for prayer that your spirit might be separated from every person with whom you have had illicit union, that you might be made free and holy to your spouse. (Matthew 16: 19, 18: 18).

Chapter 5
Understanding Yourself

Maintaining good health

Do you characteristically maintain a healthful and positive attitude and rebound from minor illnesses with quick resilience?

Physical health is definitely related to the condition of the personal spirit. Scripture speaks of this in a very concrete way:

"A man's spirit sustains him in sickness, but a crushed spirit who can bear?" (Proverbs 18: 14)

"My son, pay attention to what I say; listen closely to my words. Do not let them out of your sight, keep them within your heart; for they are life to those who find them and health to a man's whole body. Above all else, guard your heart, for it is the wellspring of life." (Proverbs 4: 20-23)

Have you noticed how some people cave in to illness? When they become sick it really gets them down. They feel their sickness deeply and they have little resilience to bounce back quickly to good health. Their illnesses seems to drag on and on.

On the other hand, there are people who seem to have indomitable spirits. They are seldom ill, and maintain a cheerful and positive demeanor even when feeling bad. They always seem to focus on the positive and are a joy to be around.

A few years ago a friend of ours attended a medical conference and shared with us later the insights he had gained from some research reports presented there. Doctors had been researching why some people of the same age, same illness, and similar life circumstances achieve quick recoveries, and others progress more slowly or do not get well at all. The result of the study indicated that the patients who achieve the quickest recovery are those who demonstrate a grateful attitude toward life.

That finding is not the least bit surprising. Remember that the spirit is the basic life force of our being. Each of us is made by God as a living creature whose body, mind, soul, and spirit are intended to be linked together in a wonderful synergy of life. When the spirit is thwarted in its development, that directly affects the body's ability to maintain physical health.

Disease is a human condition from which no one can escape. We all get sick at some time or another. And for reasons which we do not understand, even the most saintly persons are often attacked by debilitating diseases which cause suffering and death. But it is a well-documented fact that the will to live and the determination to fight disease with a positive attitude often have dramatic influence on how resistant a person is to the ravages of illness.

The vibrancy of one's personal spirit is the power source of one's will to live a positive and healthful life. If a slumbering spirit can be awakened, the body's ability to be healed or to maintain good health will greatly increase.

It is for this very reason that hospitals specializing in rehabilitation of the sick and injured employ all kinds of stimulating activities to renew the spiritual vitality of the patient. Music, reading, crafts, games, group interaction, entertainment, outings, religious services, counseling — all play a part in nurturing the spirit. These activities promote the spiritual-physical interaction in which healing can happen.

Therapists even bring pets into the rehabilitation centers to play with patients. A cute and friendly dog can do wonders to re-awaken feelings of being loved and accepted unconditionally. Cancer patients are often treated with massage therapy because the soothing touch of human hands can ease tension, renew the spirit, and stimulate both emotional and physical healing.

People who have awakened personal spirits are active, alive, enjoy life, have fun, interact with friends and family, and their very aliveness helps them to sustain good health.

Evaluate yourself! How do you feel about your general health? Do you perceive yourself as uncommonly vulnerable to illness? Are you often depressed and find it difficult to maintain a positive attitude? Do you rebound very slowly from fatigue, a cold, or the flu? If so, a slumbering spirit may be draining you of physical vitality.

Being guided by a true and working conscience

Does your personal sense of right and wrong work powerfully to alert you to moral and ethical danger areas and enable you to make good decisions to stay out of trouble ? Or, does your conscience only become active afterward to remind you that you did wrong?

This characteristic of an awakened spirit is perhaps the most important one of all because the conscience is so essential to the way we function in the world—in our relationship to God, and in our interactions with others.

There are two types of conscience—a "remorse conscience" and a "true conscience." A **remorse conscience** will be of little help to keep you out of trouble because it only works after an event to remind you that you have done wrong. It is based in flesh (a bondage to the requirements of the law and the inner man's struggle with lawless desires). A remorse conscience expresses itself primarily as "I'm sorry, I failed." A person with a remorse conscience possesses very little awareness of the specifics of how his wrongful actions may affect others. He focuses primarily on how acceptable standards of behavior were violated. A remorse conscience does not produce true repentance and does not bring one's heart to Christ so that the old self can be put to death on the cross. Consequently, a remorse conscience never leads to inner healing.

A **true conscience** works on the basis of your awakened personal spirit. It works before an event to prevent you from getting into trouble. It sings out: Warning! Warning! Warning! to alert you to the danger of temptation and the possible hurt that your wrongful actions might cause. A true conscience also can show you after an event what you have done to another person.

It can cause you to hurt empathetically for the other person's sake, not just because you have failed to uphold the law of God.

Consider for a moment how a true conscience might work. You are in a meeting with a large group of people and you see a lady sitting here who has a very nice purse. She is well dressed and would likely have quite a bit of money with her in the purse. Now suppose everyone leaves the room for a coffee break and she leaves her purse on the floor beside her chair. You are in the room by yourself. What's to keep you from stealing that purse?

The law says, "Thou shalt not steal." But the function of the law is not to keep us from sinning, is it? The law is to convict us of sin, not to empower us not to sin. Will fear stop you? Not likely! You're pretty courageous, and you're clever.

What does have the power to stop you from stealing the purse? The Lord lives in your spirit, and if your spirit is awake, the Lord gives you love for other people. Taking that woman's purse could wound her terribly. Therefore, because of your love for the Lord Jesus Christ, and because of His love singing in your spirit for her, you can't allow yourself to steal.

Another element should be mentioned here as well. Jesus said that the greatest commandment is to love our neighbor as we love ourselves. Implicit in that statement is that we should love ourselves. We should cherish our own integrity and our own high calling to Christian discipleship, so that we cannot violate ourselves by choosing a course of action that we know to be wrong.

"We know that we live in Him and He in us because He has given us His Spirit." (1 John 4: 13)

Our true conscience helps us choose what is right because the love of God sings in us. We cannot do that which is wrong because it would wound Jesus Christ and it would wound the other person. It is not for self-centered reasons that a true and working conscience will not let us sin. It is because the love of the Lord impels the conscience to think of others. It is a social conscience, born of an awakened personal spirit.

People whose spirits slumber have lessened capacity to think of how other persons will feel or how the consequences of an act might wound others. A slumbering spirit will keep a person from developing a true and working conscience even when you would least expect it, such as among Christian leaders.

This helps to understand what can happen in a situation such as those evangelists and pastors mentioned previously, who developed patterns of having sex with different women as they traveled from city to city. The Holy Spirit comes on a person, and as the Scripture says, *"a man's gift maketh room for him."* *(Proverbs 18: 16)*

He is out there preaching and teaching or evangelizing, but he has never been dealt with in the depths of his heart to heal the causes of his own slumbering spirit. The Holy Spirit has come on him and works through his mind. And the Holy Spirit works through his hands. He can preach and teach brilliantly and he can lay on hands for healing, but his own spirit is asleep.

This answers the question people have asked many times: "I thought that the very purpose of the Holy Spirit was to quicken our spirits and to bring us to life. So why aren't people like this awake if they have the Holy Spirit?"

We went to the Lord with this question and He caused us to understand it in this way:

A man can have a hardened heart in his personal spirit. Picture the Holy Spirit flowing over a man. It flows over his mind, and he preaches a beautiful sermon. It flows over his body, and he can lay on hands to heal the sick. It flows into his emotions, and he can stir the hearts of people. But picture his spirit like a boulder in the middle of a stream.

The water flows around the boulder, but it is unmoved. The water surrounds it and rushes over it, but it cannot penetrate the stone. Some people are like that. The Holy Spirit is all around them and even working through them, but they are personally unaffected in their own emotional life.

In this context, take another look at what Jesus had to say:

"Many will say to me on that day, 'Lord, Lord, did we not prophesy in your name, and in your name drive out demons and perform many miracles?' Then I will tell them plainly, 'I never knew you. Away from me, you evildoers!'"
(Matthew 7: 22, 23)

❦ **Lord,** I realize that the condition of my mind, my heart, and especially my spirit, profoundly affect the health of my body.

Search my innermost being and help me to know my sin. I ask for the gift of deep repentance. Give me the resilience of Your loving grace. Put a new and right spirit within me, Lord, and let my body reflect restored health from the inside out.

Let my conscience work before the event, whether I am tempted to sin against myself or others.

Waken my spirit so I can identify with the pain my sinful actions will afflict on God and the entire body of mankind.

Life Applications:
Understanding Yourself

1. Review the two characteristics of an awakened personal spirit listed in this chapter. Rate yourself on a scale of one to five (1= least awake, 5= most awake) by circling the degree to which you feel your spirit is in an awakened state in each.

   Maintaining good health.
      1   2   3   4   5
   Being guided by a true and working conscience.
      1   2   3   4   5

2. Now, have your spouse or a close friend rate you on the same scale without seeing your answers. How do your ratings compare?

3. How do you feel about your general health? What is the response of your heart when someone asks: "How are you doing today?" and you respond mechanically by saying, "Fine"? How do you suppose your true feelings may reflect on the condition of your personal spirit?

4. Review the two kinds of conscience described in this chapter. Which seems most characteristic of you? What actions could you take to be more sensitive to developing a true and working conscience?

5. Has the experience of rating your level of an awakened spirit been painful, enlightening, or both? What areas of spiritual slumber concern you most?

6. Share your ratings and your feelings with a Christian friend, or with your group members. What patterns do you detect in your self evaluation that reveal where you need the most re-nurturing ?

7. Talk with group members or a friend about how to help you achieve a more awakened personal spirit. Make a list of suggestions.

Pray with friends or group members about your list. Have them pray aloud with you for your spirit to be awakened.

Chapter 6
Nurturing the Spiritual Vitality of Children

Cool wind against my face
Rumpling my hair.
I am in a world apart
Hurtling along through time and space
In the back seat of the family car
Snuggled close against my mother.
I feel her warmth—her hand in mine.
I quietly explore the texture of her skin,
The subtle veins, the gently curving palm.
I trace the life-lines
Appearing and disappearing.
The hard edge of fingernails.
Softness and strength.
Mostly, I am wondering at the meaning
Of mothers and fathers and families.
Of hands and of touching
And of love.
Sitting close as we speed along
Into the night
Holding hands and wondering
How marvelous this is.
This touching—This simple delight.
— Norm Bowman

Spiritual nurture is our way of bringing young lives into a conscious awareness of a loving God. It is a step-by-step, day-by-day celebration of how we are connected to each other, to the world around us, and to God who is the creator and sustainer of all life.

We do not create the spirit by our nurture. We only provide the loving, fertile environment in which the spirit can unfold naturally in a child. Our personal spirit is the breath of life within us. The Hebrew word *ruach* and the Greek word *pneuma* are the words used for this breath or wind from God that flows through us to give us life. To be an agent of healthy nurture is to stay attuned to the natural wonder of a child's discovery and enthusiasm for all of life—to encourage emotional sensitivity and expression, not to discourage and stifle it.

---

*The quality of our nurture
is the single most important element affecting
the future spiritual and mental health and
wholeness of our children.*

It is difficult to stay focused on the wonder and responsibility of spiritual nurture when so much of our daily life is measured in seemingly ordinary moments. This is particularly true amid the stress of nightly awakenings, diaper changes, dirty dishes, and endless hours of rocking a colicky baby. But what we do with and for our children, particularly from the time of birth till the age of six, will have a lasting impact on the rest of their lives.

The following are key concepts of spiritual nurturing:
- ◆ Building trust by much affectionate touch
- ◆ Establishing loving discipline
- ◆ Staying open to the wonder of discovery
- ◆ Building a supportive family life
- ◆ Teaching and modeling attitudes and behavior
- ◆ Talking so kids will listen

❧ Building Trust

A baby learns trust by feeling secure. This comes through being gently and carefully held, touched, snuggled, loved and played with. Infants need this physical contact to begin to develop that connectedness with other people beyond themselves and their mother. Ideally, this affectionate cuddling should come both from parents and other family members. But the father, as mentioned previously, has a special responsibility as he assumes his God-given role as parent and co-nurturer.

Some fathers, whether out of fear of not knowing what to do or out of misplaced role modeling, admire their children from a distance but leave the physical care of the baby to the mother. Fathers should be aware that babies need their attention and their loving touch. A baby needs the father's presence and attentive nurture to build the simple trust and first feelings of corporateness essential to an awakened personal spirit.

On the other hand, some fathers in the exuberance of young parenthood are tempted to become a little too active with their newborn baby in an attempt to play. Wild swinging to and fro, throwing the baby into the air and catching him, or dropping him suddenly and catching him in mid-fall may seem like fun and will definitely get a response from a child. But these kinds of severe actions with a baby are not likely to build the kind of security and trust an infant needs to develop.

Gentle rocking while being securely held and other non-threatening stimulation is more in order. As the child grows and becomes more responsive and playful, he will naturally let you know when he is ready for more adventurous fun.

As a baby moves from infancy into childhood, trust takes on a broader meaning. Touching is still important and play time is a natural expression of that physical intimacy. But children also need to feel secure in their parents' love as expressed in other ways. Being present, being attentive, being consistent, and being unselfishly fair are the basic ingredients that build trust in a child.

♦ A child who loses a grandparent or even a pet to death may need a lot of reassurance that you too are not going to desert him in some way.

♦ A child whose parents separate or divorce needs a lot of special attention to overcome the insecurity of loss, and to understand that his parents' problems are not his fault. If more parents understood the negative impact divorce can have on their children, perhaps they would work harder to salvage their marriage relationship for the sake of their children's welfare.

♦ A child who has two very busy working parents needs special times of very focused attention with them to overcome the feeling of being an unimportant person in a busy world. A child needs to be able to trust in the knowledge that he is supremely important to the people who love him.

♦ A child needs to be able to trust his parents to be consistently believable. He needs promises to be kept, and discipline to be administered consistently; he needs to observe his parents practicing what they preach.

❦ Establishing Loving Discipline

Discipline is an essential element in child rearing, but there is a distinct line between appropriately administered spankings to correct dangerous or inappropriate behavior and the repeated intimidation and violent spankings that are abusive.

Common sense should tell us that a newborn baby should not be treated in the same way you would treat an older child who has reached the age of accountability. A baby is not a reasoning person who makes willful decisions to disobey. A baby cries when he is hungry, uncomfortable, or in pain and needs to be lovingly tended to reduce his discomfort. Spanking, shaking, angry shouting, or other kinds of physical coercion in an attempt to discipline a baby for crying has absolutely no place in healthy nurturing. During this stage of development a child is not willfully disobeying and has no ability to understand the reason for such action. He can respond only with more discomfort, confusion, and insecurity — and his personal spirit will be suppressed.

Unfortunately, many people have grown up in homes in which spanking of young babies and severe whipping of children was a common practice. Unless they can be brought to a more enlightened understanding, such parenting techniques are passed from one generation to another even when they are wrong and emotionally destructive.

When a child is old enough to explore his world by climbing under, around, and over everything in sight, the concept of discipline begins to take on legitimacy. Developmentally, the child can begin to learn cause and effect relationships, and appropriate discipline can begin the teaching of limits. The meaning of "No" can be reinforced by physically restraining a child from reaching for a dangerous object or going where he is not allowed. Although language comprehension is at a rudimentary level, a spanking of the hands accompanied by a firm "No" will begin to make an impression and establish needed limits on a child's behavior.

A typical example of this was when our grandson Joel first discovered that he could crawl into the bathroom and play with that wonderful roll of toilet paper. His first delight was to grab one end and crawl down the hall with the paper trailing off the spindle in a stream behind him. We all laughed, of course, and thought, "How cute!" However, the cuteness turned to trouble when Joel learned to reel off great armloads and dump it into the toilet until the bowl would become clogged.

Mother Victoria's initial scoldings were an ineffective deterrent, so she began to slap his little hands each time he would begin the toilet paper tearing. Although he could only talk in one or two word phrases, he soon got the point—"Throwing paper in the bowl makes mommy angry and gets my hands slapped." Joel showed us in a vividly non-verbal way that he was learning the lesson. One day after watching him crawl down the hall toward the bathroom, Victoria went to see what he was doing. Joel had cleverly closed the bathroom door. Inside she found him standing beside the stool, pulling at the toilet paper roll. When he turned around to see her watching, he held out one of his little hands and spanked himself just as his mother had done! An early lesson in learning limits.

As a child grows older and the mind is more capable of weighing right against wrong and its consequences, discipline in its various forms can take on additional significance. Privileges, such as having special treats, watching TV, or play time with friends, can be a reward for good behavior and can be withheld as a consequence of disobedience. Children need to learn in simple ways that they must bear responsibility for their actions and that decisions to disobey will result in predictable consequences.

I (Paula) remember being disciplined in many creative ways by my mother. I remember most clearly the times I misbehaved and my mother would send me to the back yard to cut a switch off the tree with which I would be whacked several times across the back of my legs. Yes, the spankings always hurt enough to get my attention, but it was the trip to the back yard and the cutting of my own switch that I find indelibly printed in my mind. In retrospect, I think my being sent to cut my own switch served two distinct purposes.

That trip to the back yard always gave me time to pause and ponder what I had done and the consequences I was to suffer. The trip reinforced in my mind what my mother's expectations were. It also gave my mother time to cool down and not spank me in anger. I would always get the spanking but it was from a more collected mom who could calmly explain just why I was being disciplined and who would express her love and support for me following the punishment.

The Scripture speaks of the need for discipline and even of the appropriateness of a spanking when needed.

"He who spares the rod hates his son, but he who loves him is careful to discipline him." (Proverbs 13: 24)

"Fathers, do not provoke your children to anger, but bring them up in the discipline and instruction of the Lord." (Ephesians 6: 4)

"Do not withhold discipline from a child; if you punish him with the rod, he will not die. Punish him with the rod and save his soul from death." (Proverbs 23: 13-14)

Discipline, and especially a spanking, should always be followed with expressions of love. Think of it this way. If discipline is administered to you without love, it means that your soul is being hauled to account, your mind is hauled to account, and your emotions are pulled up short. Discipline by itself may bring you under control, but your spirit is likely to retreat and sit sullenly in a hole. You may come back into the family to participate, but not all of you would be there. Your spirit will stay in retreat or be provoked to resentment and anger.

If discipline is followed by expressions of love and hugs, then your spirit is drawn out again to be part of the family and to want to be there. This teaches the child that discipline and love go together.

A child needs to understand that discipline is for his own good and it costs the parent pain to do it. Children need to experience loving touch right after discipline. There are several things about loving discipline that should be remembered.

Never cause more pain than the infraction deserves.

Discipline may include an occasional spanking to establish consequences for dangerous or inappropriate behaviors. But severe spankings or any other kind of physical violence which inflicts bruises, cuts, or other tissue damage to a child is clearly abusive and ceases to produce the character formation desired.

Similarly, a child can benefit from verbal reprimand, but constant verbal attack and its subsequent emotional trauma is also abusive and counter-productive to a child's healthy nurture. When a child is continually called stupid or told he is a bad person, his self concept will suffer. He will begin to believe it and his spirit will be stifled.

For toddlers who have a well-developed understanding of language, and are able to remember their transgressions, the loss of a privilege may be a more effective way to discipline. For instance, two-year-old Briana loves to watch Walt Disney movies. She resists going to bed at night. Persistent disobedience is usually stopped when she is firmly told, "If you get out of your bed one more time, you will not be allowed to watch your movie tomorrow."

Effective discipline requires consistency, firmness, and love.

Consistency of discipline is important so as not to confuse a child. If a reprimand or spanking is given for an offense on one occasion and then overlooked the next time, the lesson will hold little value for a child. Parents, teachers, and caretakers should make their expectations very clear; otherwise the child will have no sense of what the boundaries are.

Loving discipline achieves its effects without fear.

Loving discipline preserves the integrity of the spirit and allows a child to learn the lesson and bounce back without the lingering impact of fear. Punishment produces fear, but discipline allows us to grow strong. This is an important lesson in building strong character in children. Through loving discipline, they learn to take rebuke, yet still retain the security that they will continue to be loved. Later in life when setbacks befall them, they will have the strength of character to accept the responsibility for their wrongs, take whatever comes, and know that they are OK.

"Our fathers disciplined us for a little while as they thought best; but God disciplines us for our good, that we may share in his holiness." (Hebrews 12: 10)

🍎 Staying Open to the Wonder of Discovery

As we become more open to the life-giving energy that flows naturally from children, we cannot help but be transformed in many ways as well. We grow alongside children, and if we allow ourselves, we learn to freely play again and discover a rebirth of joy and delight that may have fallen asleep within us years ago. For adults preoccupied with an adult world and the pressures of career and home, this can be a difficult transition.

Carol Bowman (Norm's wife) tells of a dream she had during the late stages of pregnancy with their son, Matthew. She was an account executive for a major insurance company and traveled frequently, dealing professionally with executives in government agencies. In her dream she saw herself in the hospital giving birth to her son. When the nurses brought the baby to her for the first time, they sat him down on her chest. He was dressed in a three-piece business suit, carried a junior-sized briefcase, and began a conversation with her.

Absurd? Perhaps. But her subconscious mind threw up a role conflict image that is common to many parents. Fortunately, in real life, her new role of nurturing mother came very easily. The ensuing months of quiet time, snuggling, playing with and nurturing her baby became the happiest and most richly rewarding times of her life.

The point is that babies and very young children aren't just junior adults and cannot be treated as such. They need the time and attention of parents and family members who will get down on the floor and play with them on their developmental level, lovingly and gently helping them to explore their new environment and to keep open the wonder of new life unfolding.

Helping children stay open to the wonder of discovery doesn't have to be a chore. It mostly means paying attention to what interests and excites them at each developmental stage of their life and trying not to stifle that natural curiosity and sense of good fun.

Instead of saying "No," lest children get themselves dirty or interrupt your hurry to get to the next place you are rushing to, take the time to let them splash in the puddle, look at the bug, or watch the sparrows sitting on the telephone line.

If you want to organize their wonder of discovery into more regimented activities to fit your day, you might try paying attention to how you can make an adventure out of such things as meal time, bath time, bed time, chore time, and play time. Or try starting meaningful family rituals or traditions. Here are a few suggestions to get your mind churning:

Meal Time

♦ Let kids get involved in the meal by helping to peel the potatoes or carrots, stir the soup, sprinkle in the seasoning, set the table. Make a nest in their mashed potatoes for green pea eggs. Make their hot cakes in the shape of hearts or crescent moons. Let them make smiley faces with mustard on their sandwiches. Ask their advice on how to cook. Let it be a learning experience.

♦ Kids love romance and the unusual. Occasionally try mealtime as a formal occasion. Let them make place cards for seating. Try eating by candlelight. Ring a bell for the "waiter" to pass you seconds. On other occasions spread a blanket on the floor and make the meal a picnic.

♦ Have an occasional "Cave Man Meal" in which it is OK for everyone to eat with their fingers. Serve the food on plastic wrap with no utensils. Maybe it will help them appreciate the practicality of plates, forks and good manners.

Bath Time

♦ Fun bath time is when a child can take whatever toys he or she wants to the tub and stay as long as desired. If kids get fussy when the water gets cold, show them how to warm it up. If they balk at washing hair, let them do it with swimming goggles on to keep the soap out of their eyes.

♦ Romantic bath time can be by candlelight with bubbles and a tape or radio playing classical music. Or, put in a favorite music tape and sing-along.

Bed Time

♦ If you are always short of time and in a hurry to get kids to bed, try reading the bedtime story while your kid is in the bathtub.

♦ Record yourself reading a favorite bed time story. Then let the child take the tape recorder and book to bed alone and follow along in the book to your recorded voice.

Chore Time

♦ Try to make household chores fun. Suggest that kids pretend that dirt is the bad guy. Let them use squirt guns to spray window cleaner and then capture the bad guy by wiping dry with a paper towel.

♦ Most kids love to polish. Let them shine up the silverware, or dust and polish the dining table.

♦ Give kids a choice among several chores they would like to do — vacuum carpets, dust furniture, fold clothes, etc. Work alongside them to instruct and to praise jobs well done — and for the fun of fellowship.

Play Time

♦ Go for a neighborhood nature walk. Let kids take paper bags and pick up anything from nature they find interesting. Talk about the objects as they are found, or afterwards at home. Emphasize the beauty of God's creation. Start a collection. Be careful not to superimpose your value judgment on what objects hold wonder. Their interests may be quite different from yours and should be cherished, understood and talked about.

♦ Save old and unusual clothes, shoes, and hats for a dress-up box. Have a weekly dress-up and pretend time. Encourage yours and the neighborhood kids to dress up and make up a play about their imaginary characters.

♦ Help children write letters to the authors of their favorite story book. Chances are good that they will get a nice reply.

♦ Organize a field trip to take several children to an interesting place like a local bakery, fire station, factory, etc.

Family Rituals

♦ Always hold hands in family unity to say grace before meals. (You might even try sitting down at the dining table for meals instead of eating in front of the TV.)

♦ Make a daily "Hug Sandwich" with adults on the outside and kids in the middle as the peanut butter and jelly, all squeezing together.

♦ Encourage children to help put a family photo album together and add to it regularly. Tell them your family history. Show them photos of your ancestors so they can recognize and tell stories about them. This builds a sense of roots, of personal history and belonging.

♦ Establish a ritual of blessing your children each morning before they go off to school. Stop them at the door or in the car before they get out. Place your hands on them and pray something similar to this: "Dear God, we ask your blessing today on this Your child. Help him to have a wonderful and happy learning experience at school. Help him do his very best. Keep him safe from harm. We bless him now with our love in Jesus' name, Amen."

🐛 Building a Supportive Family Life

If a child is to grow up with ability to love, empathize and relate to others in a responsible way, he must learn what it is to live in community with others. This begins with parents — first in intimacy with the mother, then in contact with the outside world, hopefully with a loving and nurturing father. Beyond that, a child greatly benefits in being surrounded by an extended family of brothers and sisters, cousins, aunts and uncles, and close family friends. These important persons become extensions of the child's self. If a primary family exists to surround the child with this community of love, nurturing of the child should be encouraged by creating opportunities for the entire family to come together and share.

The reality of our world is that many children are born into single parent homes or in homes that have a limited natural support system of grandparents or other blood relatives who live nearby. If this is the case, a nurturing parent should look for every opportunity to develop a network of loving friends who can become an important source of support for a growing child.

Increasing numbers of aware Christians are responding to this need. The church is still the best place for parents to find the quality of nurture children require. Look for caring, loving friends to become your "family" through Sunday school classes, Bible study groups, and in home prayer groups.

Be a friend and make friends.
Share of yourself and let others into your life. Ask for
their commitment to help you and your child grow. This
is what the church should be.

A child who lives in a family context will begin to pick up at a very early age what it is to belong. The family doing things together builds a sense of identity and belonging in the spirit of the child. From peek-a-boo to patty-cake, the happy interaction of child and siblings and adult relatives begins to nurture a powerful sense of community.

Jean Grasso Fitzpatrick in her wonderfully insightful book titled *Something More, Nurturing Your Child's Spiritual Growth*, refers to three strong functions of the family as a nurturing community.

First — the family is a living embodiment of what it means to be spiritual; to have a place in community, to value people more than things, and to be sustained by sacred bonds of relationships.

Second — the family functions as a community of memory; children see their own lives in the context of family stories and events and they begin to understand how they and their family relate to the broader context of society.

Third — the home gives children a perspective on the wider world; it sets the example for relating in ministry or acting with justice toward others in the extended human family.

Children are very impressionable and often become nostalgic about what their families do at special times of celebration, whether it be an event such as a marriage, a holiday, or even a family reunion. "What was it like when you got married, Mom and Dad?" "Tell us how Grandpa used to cut down and decorate the Christmas tree." "What did your family do on Thanksgiving when you were a little girl, Aunt Barbara?"

Take care to make holidays special occasions when the family is together. And even more than that, celebrate the significance of holidays by talking about or acting out the reason for the event.

As children grow and begin to comprehend the meaning of special events, take time to discuss what we are thankful for on Thanksgiving and spend family time together in prayer. Hang out the flag and visit a cemetery on Memorial Day, and make an object lesson of why we remember those who gave their lives to secure our freedom and our peace. With a nativity scene, act out the events surrounding Jesus' birth on Christmas Day. Explain how gift exchanges are our way of responding to the gift God gave the world by sending His Son. Make real the awful events and meaning of Good Friday and the wonderful Easter message of the raising of Jesus from the dead.

On every possible occasion, share as a family. Sit together at meals. Eat, talk, play, and sing together. Family togetherness builds ability within the spirit to be open, to relate, and to function in corporateness.

❧ Teaching and Modeling Attitudes and Behavior

I (John) can remember my mother's words ringing in my ears. "Jackie, a gentleman never curses in front of a lady, or any other time." "Jackie, a man never hits a woman. Any man who hits a woman is no man at all." "Jackie, a gentleman treats his wife with courtesy and respect at all times. He never insults her or hurts her. He treats her like a lady at all times."

That teaching might have found no lodging place in me, had I not seen my father model it in his own life. Children learn what you model, more than what you say. I never heard my father raise his voice to my mother or say an insulting or cross word to her. I heard him and saw him treat her with respect at all times. I saw affection from him to her continually. And those lessons, modeled by my parents, have been written in my heart.

If you don't want your child to lie, cheat on tests at school, or steal from friends, begin by paying attention to how fairly you deal with business clients, how much integrity you show in abiding by the law, and how honest you are about taking advantage of other people or their property. If you don't want your children to drink or take drugs, pay attention to the example you are setting for them. It's not enough to say, "Some things are for adults, and when you are old enough this will be OK." Very simply, practice what you preach, or don't be surprised when your children pick up on your worst habits. If you are concerned enough about setting the right example for your child to change your questionable behavior, your changed behavior will reap positive benefits in your life as well.

❦ Talking So Kids Will Listen

Effective communication is an essential ingredient in keeping the personal spirit alive in children as they grow older. Good communication skills are a learned behavior and require a concerted effort to remain open and effective.

Adele Faber and Elaine Mazlish have written a wonderfully helpful guidebook for parents with the title *How to Talk So Kids Will Listen & Listen So Kids Will Talk.* The principles taught in this book are not particularly new, although the book has enlightened thousands of parenting study groups and revolutionized communication within thousands of families in recent years. What Faber and Mazlish teach are common sense approaches to helping parent-child communication stay open and constructive rather than closed and repressive.

All of us as parents, teachers, or family members should consider carefully how we relate to children in daily conversation. Does our conversation impart the positive support and nurture they need to stay vibrantly alive in their spirits? Or does our constant critical and judgmental attitude cause them to retreat into woundedness?

The following overview of ways to more openly communicate with children should be helpful to avoid falling into the trap of judgment and criticism: (For further insight into many kinds of communication skills, we recommend the study of *How to Talk So Kids Will Listen & Listen So Kids Will Talk*.)

◆ **Pay attention to what children have to say.** Take the time to listen quietly and attentively.

◆ **Acknowledge the reality of children's feelings.** Even though you may not like the mode of delivery, do not try to deny a child the honest expression of that emotion.

◆ **Help children identify feelings by giving the feelings a name or description.** For example: "What I hear is that you get very angry when you are treated that way;" or perhaps, "Getting a good grade on your test today certainly has put you in a happy mood this afternoon."

◆ **When you discover a problem, avoid heavy or repetitive scolding.** Rather, simply describe what you see, to call it to their attention. For example: "I see you chose not to clean your room this morning. I hope you understand it must be done before you go out this afternoon."

◆ **Give enough information so an event can be understood as to why it is a problem.** For example: "I don't want you to come in the kitchen on roller skates because the rollers will damage the tile floor. Do you understand?"

♦ **Be brief and to the point in communicating your desire—even as brief as one word to call attention to a problem that has been discussed previously.** For example, when the child appears at the kitchen door with roller skates on, simply say, "The skates." (But say it lightly; they will pick up on every ounce of irritation or condemnation.)

♦ **Clearly communicate to children the expectations of what you consider to be acceptable and unacceptable behavior.** They need to know what the boundaries are.

♦ **Describe how you feel to children — what you like and what you don't like.** For example: "I like it when you remember to tell me where you are going and when you will return;" or perhaps, "It makes me angry to think that you deliberately disobeyed my instructions."

♦ **Give children a choice between options to avoid rigid confrontations and to help them develop autonomy.** For example: "Which do you prefer? Stay home and go to the party or go on the camping trip?" Or, "Which outfit will you wear, your coat with a tie or white shirt and sweater?"

♦ **Show respect for the ways children struggle to solve problems, make decisions, or learn by experience.** For example: "I know it must have been hard for you not to argue with your teacher when you felt falsely accused, but you showed maturity in making that decision."

◆ **Encourage children with helpful advice rather than taking over and doing things for them.** For example: "When you fry bacon, try turning the fire down lower so it will cook more slowly. Then it will be less likely to burn."

◆ **Don't ask too many questions to probe for information.** Encourage discussion with open-ended statements like: "Tell me about your day." With younger children, be more specific to help them find descriptive words.

◆ **Don't rush to answer children's questions as though you are always the authority.** Rather, ask them what they think to help sharpen their problem-solving skills and turn the question into a two-way discussion.

◆ **Encourage children to include sources outside the home for information.** Help them experience research to discover needed information. For example: "Why don't we stop at the pet store so you can ask them what they think is the best way to housebreak a new puppy?"

◆ **Don't take away hope by discouraging new experiences or activities that might stretch a child's ability.** For example: "It may be tough to make the team because you are younger than the other boys, but trying out will be good experience whether you make it or not."

◆ **Call attention to the positive things you observe.** Give praise when deserved. For example: "I saw how you responded positively to the coach's criticism of your play today. You were careful to do it better the next time. You're becoming a good athlete because you're coachable."

♦ **Describe what you see when you observe positive behavior.** For example: "I see you did all your chores this morning. Now you'll have the rest of the day to do whatever you like."

♦ **Describe how you feel when you are pleased or proud.** For example: "I was so proud of you today, the way you set a good example for the younger children who were looking up to you."

♦ **Model the behavior you would like to see in a child.** For example: "I cleaned out the garage today and have several things to donate to the Salvation Army thrift store. Would you like to donate some of the toys you don't play with any more so some other children might enjoy them?"

Basic elements essential to the development of a healthy and awakened personal spirit in a child are really very simple. Despite the pressures that are a normal part of any household, children need affectionate touch, the loving presence of a family, focused time with good communication, guided exploration, gentle discipline, and the warmth of love.

❦ Lord, write it on my heart that I will never in all my life have an opportunity to influence a life so profoundly as I will the children you have placed under my care.

Equip me with a listening ear, an understanding and loving heart, arms that embrace with clean, wholesome affection, and a tongue which praises and encourages.

Give me Your wisdom to discipline consistently and appropriately with unconditional love.

Make me an attractive model for joyful adventure in discovering the wonders of God's creation.

Life Applications: Nurturing the Spiritual Vitality of Children

Significant strides can be made in effective nurturing of children if husbands and wives will stay focused, be consistent in promoting a balanced and stimulating lifestyle and regularly talk about how to work at it together.

Review the six suggested nurturing areas in this chapter. Then duplicate the outline below to structure one focused activity in each area that you will schedule and practice during each week. Use this list as a daily reminder of ways to improve your ability to nurture a child's developing personal spirit.

Begin keeping a daily journal of thoughts, feelings, activities, successes, failures, and memorable experiences you have with your child. Let your journal help you grow daily in spiritual vitality along with your child.

Weekly "Child Nurturing" Activities & Awarenesses

1. Ways I can build trust:

2. Ways I can establish loving discipline:

3. Ways I can help children stay open to the wonder of discovery:

4. Ways I can help to build a supportive family life:

5. Ways in which I can discipline myself to teach and model behavior better than I have in the past:

6. Ways I can improve family communication by talking so kids will listen, and listening so kids will talk:

Chapter 7
Rise and Shine:
Re-Awakening Your Spirit

How fragile are the lines that give us life.
How short the stems — how delicate the leaves.
How subject to the winds
Of chance and circumstance.
We come into the world like seeds spilled
Randomly along the way.
Naked and alone, dependent on the soil of fortune
For food and warmth and nurture.
We rise from our beginnings, gasping for air
Reaching out for love and care
Moved internally by life forces
Beyond our knowing.
How powerful are the lessons learned
That living builds on living
Strength breeds strength
Care nurtures care
Love reaps love
Hope follows hope
And growing is a choosing.
Down within us all
There is resilience called the grace of God.
It takes the fear from fragileness
And gives vibrancy to life.
Death is real — It stalks us daily
And walks with certain ugly pride.
But there is another side.
Beyond the darkness is the light of life.

— Norm Bowman

One cannot expect to awaken the personal spirit simply by awareness that the problem exists. This is perhaps a misconception born out of the way some psychoanalytical counseling is practiced — that if one becomes adequately aware of a problem, the self-awareness will naturally result in a solution and healing.

Healing is not a simple process. Oftentimes there are complex issues which stand as obstacles within an individual to complicate one's functioning in a healthy and spiritually alive state. Unfortunately, many people suffer from clinical depression or manic-depressive mood swings which appear to be caused by chemical imbalances in the body. With competent diagnosis from a physician, these can be treated very effectively with medication to restore an emotional equilibrium.

Many others suffer from debilitating diseases, chronic pain, or psychiatric disorders which must be addressed as very real problems requiring a combination of medical treatment and spiritual therapy to produce healing or to allow one to adequately cope with physical or mental problems. As stated earlier, we must view ourselves in a wholistic way as beings created by God in an interrelated combination of body, spirit, soul and mind. God works in and through the medical profession to provide keys to restoring physical and mental health. We should not downplay the importance of that source of help as we seek wholeness of body as well as the spiritual vitality God desires for us.

The first step in seeking the revitalization of your personal spirit is to evaluate whether you have any serious physical or mental conditions which stand as obstacles to achieving vitality in your personal spirit. Seek medical help and accept the mature counsel of professionals to realistically evaluate your condition and how you may best receive treatment. Then focus on ways you can seek a re-awakening of your personal spirit to contribute to an integrated wholeness of body, mind and spirit.

Your personal spirit slumbers because you have experienced a wounding or anesthetizing of your precious life energy. To awaken the personal spirit, you must go through a process of both healing and re-nurturing.

The healing process entails working through forgiveness toward those who either wounded you and/or neglected to give the nurture your spirit required. Then you must experience a process of nurture that will awaken the spirit and rejuvenate it so that you may become more and more human.

For an adult, re-nurturing your personal spirit is a choosing process. It is not something someone else can do for you. Nor is it something for which you can count on God for a quick miracle, or that will be "instantly fixed" by prayer.

You cannot change what you do not recognize and acknowledge. You must want to change and you must be willing to seek and accept the loving nurture that can awaken your spirit.

In the fifth and sixth chapter of his letter to the Ephesian church, Paul gave a wonderfully concise list of positive actions Christians should take to come into the fullness of life in Jesus Christ. We mentioned these earlier but they bear repeating in paraphrased form. Follow these admonitions and you will have taken the first series of steps on a journey toward wholeness of your personal spirit.

♦ Be careful and choose wisely how you will live. *(Ephesians 5: 15)*

♦ Find out what pleases the Lord and be imitators of Christ. *(Ephesians 5: 17)*

♦ Stay away from intoxicants that will drug your senses and make you susceptible to immorality. *(Ephesians 5: 18)*

♦ Seek opportunities to relate to others light-heartedly, with laughter, singing, and spirit-filled fun. *(Ephesians 5: 19)*

♦ Give thanks to God for everything life brings. *(Ephesians 5: 20)*

♦ Submit to each other in love and trust as Christian brothers and sisters. *(Ephesians 5: 21)*

♦ Be honorable in your family relations by treating others with respect and consideration. *(Ephesians 6: 1-4)*

♦ Seek the Lord for strength, nurture, and cherishing. Be confident in His power to nurture and protect you. *(Ephesians 6: 10-12)*

The process of re-awakening your personal spirit cannot be accomplished by yourself. You must have help from others. Even if you are seeking help through a professional counselor, it is unlikely that the healing and nurture can happen adequately in that one-on-one relationship. The awakening of the spirit happens best and most effectively through sharing relationships within a small group.

Slumbering spirits need friends who will love them back to life. With this in mind, we give the following suggestions about seeking an awakening of your personal spirit and how to sustain your spirit as a vital life force.

Explore ways in which your spirit may be asleep.

Be aware of your shortcomings and the areas of your life in which you are experiencing difficulty. Take inventory of your feelings and behavior to evaluate what kinds of activities prompt the most excitement and aliveness in you and what activities generate little interest. How many of the following questions can you answer affirmatively?

◆ When talking with others, do you understand and communicate with them on a feeling level, or do you have to think and choose your words carefully to know what to say?

◆ Do you easily empathize with your friends? Can you weep with their sadness and share their rejoicing, or only respond intellectually?

◆ Are you able to sustain close relationships with people over a long period of time?

◆ Are you enjoying life and participating fully with others in activities that are fun?

◆ Do you have a good sense of humor?

◆ Do you feel close to God? Are you able to bask in His presence both in corporate worship and in private devotions, or do you experience God distantly just as an act of faith?

◆ Do you feel spiritually alive?

◆ Is sex with your spouse a holy meeting, or merely pleasurable sensations that might be just as good with someone else?

◆ Does inspiration come quickly and easily for you with new ideas and thoughts?

◆ Do you thrill to good music and art, or does it just leave you unmoved and uninterested?

◆ Does your conscience sing out forcibly before an event, or only remind you afterwards that you should not have done something?

◆ Do you feel vibrantly alive and refreshed by being out in nature, or is a walk in nature as flat in feeling as other experiences?

Make a list of the areas of your life where you feel most asleep and which you would like to rejuvenate. Thoughtfully review the nurturing relationships you have had with parents and significant others in your growing up years.

For best effect, discuss these issues with a close friend, or share within a small group among those who understand why you are seeking an awakening of your personal spirit.

♦ What were your parents like?

♦ How close did you feel to them while growing up?

♦ How physically expressive of love were your parents and other family members ?

♦ In what ways did they support and encourage you?

♦ To what degree did they communicate vibrancy of life to you?

♦ What relationship do you have with your parents now?

♦ In what ways do you harbor ill will, anger, or regrets? (You may have more than you are aware of, but list those you recognize in yourself.)

♦ How willing are you to move beyond the past to for-give those who may have hurt you?

♦ How badly do you want to have a more fully awakened personal spirit?

❧ Seek affection in your own family.

Seeking affection from parents or close relatives may be dif-ficult if they have been part of the problem in the past. But a re-newed effort to build more intimate relationships with family members is always in order. This can include talking that goes beyond the standard chit chat about TV shows, the weather, or the day's shopping expedition. Be more aware of how you share feelings and speak from the heart in your conversations.

It may be frustrating to try to draw feelings out of others (particularly family members) who are not accustomed to shar-ing in this way. Do something special: write a note, send a card, phone for no reason, take the opportunity to pay someone a compliment. You cannot be responsible for their unwillingness to respond with affection. Neither can you allow yourself to harbor anger for their inabilities. But you can be more open yourself and more willing to be vulnerable. And you can practice asking the kind of open and non-threatening questions of others that will give them an opportunity to share.

Deepening your relationships also means paying attention to how you can express affection in more physical ways. Make a major effort to overcome any resistance you may have to giving and receiving hugs, holding hands, sitting close to others, or engaging in quiet focused conversations that are uninterrupted by the TV, radio, or household duties. In small ways like this, your spirit can be refreshed and come to new levels of wakefulness.

Discuss with parents, brothers, sisters, aunts, uncles and children the ways in which your family expresses affection or fails to express affection. If expressions of affection are lacking, encourage them to be more demonstrative physically. Ask for a hug. Embrace each other when greeting or parting. Hold hands to pray at special family gatherings or at mealtime. Try an occasional group hug or sing a song together as a family as you stand in a circle with your arms around each other's shoulders. Begin to make those kinds of touching experiences a ritual of loving care. Some family members may not be able to do this. Their spirits are too deeply asleep, but you will have tried.

❦ Identify with Christian friends who will understand, support, and confront you in love.

A wise counselor will recommend and arrange for the person he or she is counseling to get involved in a small group to help with the healing and growth process. If this doesn't happen, start a group yourself. You don't have to make a big project of it. Ask among Christian friends with whom you have prayed or would like to pray. Invite them over for coffee or for dinner. Ask if they would be interested in joining a group in which members share, pray, love, and support one another. Then just begin.

If this seems to be difficult for you, remember the old adage that to have a friend you must be a friend. This holds true with Christian friends as well. Building relationships requires presence, openness, and patience.

So often a person visits a church almost expecting to be rejected — with the attitude that the people met there must meet certain standards in order to prove that they are friendly and accepting. Then when the church people don't take the "proper" initiative, you can say that they were an unfriendly group and you wouldn't have been happy there after all.

Granted, the church is full of cliques, hypocrites, and sinners. But so is the world, only more so. The church still remains the most likely place to find people who will love you, accept you, and help you become your best self.

A little known short-cut to getting what you want is to ask for it. If people have to guess your needs, it makes knowing you a task, and you are less likely to receive the kind of response that will help heal your wounded spirit. Keep trying until you find that combination of friends who can really click together. Be patient but persistent. Not everyone is ready for the kind of sharing that can happen in the dynamics of a small group. But remember too, that there are a lot of people in the world just like you who have the same kinds of life concerns, and the same desires to grow in the Lord and to come alive in their spirits.

It often happens that a small group of close friends will help its members to become more awakened in their personal spirits just by getting together and expressing love to each other. Ideally, however, the group will be much more effective if they are informed about inner healing and understand the concept of the slumbering spirit. So much more can be done if the group understands the specific kinds of needs an individual has and is familiar with ways to encourage one's spirit to come alive.

❦ Lighten your heart through good clean fun.

Play as much as possible and seek opportunities for enjoyment and recreation. Read uplifting books. Choose books of heroism, inspiration, fantasy, and lofty values — even childhood fantasy books which will restore lost child-like qualities. Go to see inspiring movies (although those seem to be more difficult to find these days). Avoid the mindless violence, sexploitation, and action thrillers. Rather, seek out the classic stories, old and new, that are uplifting to the spirit and portray heroism, love, indomitable spirits, and good comedic fun.

Let yourself laugh, even with slapstick foolishness. And let yourself cry when you are moved by poignant tales. Your spirit thrives on healthy expressions of emotion.

---

*Play with your children, nieces, nephews, or
neighborhood kids. Let the child inside you
come out to enjoy the simple kinds of
play activities that give children pleasure.*

We have a friend who tells how her daughter helped her come alive to the childish joy that had been buried so deeply within her. For several years she found herself dreading her child's appeals to take her to the playground. She would often go begrudgingly and just watch. But with her daughter's insistence she began to enter in more readily — to swing on the swing set and to push and ride the merry-go-round. The playful activity and sharing in her daughter's joy began to loosen her up emotionally. Soon she began to look forward to the experience. It became refreshing and energizing to her and she began to discover a new openness and excitement about the small things in her world that previously had gone unnoticed.

Don't take life so seriously. Be kind and nurture yourself with fun activities. Go back to chapter 6 and review some of the activities you can do with children. Put yourself in the place of a child and do these activities for yourself. (Go ahead. Take a bath by candlelight, or with goggles on to keep the soap out of your eyes. Why not?)

Get together often with Christian friends. Seek out companionship for talking, sharing, singing, laughing, and playing together. Be real. Be alive.

Take an interest in each others' families. Expand the circle of your love. Pay attention to little things. Take time to celebrate birthdays, anniversaries, special days, accomplishments. Talk to each other regularly on the phone if you do not have opportunity to meet in person.

Do kind things for each other. Surprise your friends with a pie or cake, or share a recipe. Recommend and share a good book. Ask for advice or a referral to a doctor. Be friendly and be a friend.

Husbands and wives, pour all of your affection out to one another, warmly and openly. It will affirm and revitalize each of you. Give joyously and adventurously to each other in your sex life; it will increase your intimacy and help you come alive.

 Take care of yourself with plenty of sleep, exercise and maintain a healthy diet.

Doctors frequently recommend that patients suffering from stress and nervous tension get regular exercise and become involved in an enjoyable recreational activity. That's good advice for the slumbering spirit as well. Get active in a sport or a hobby.

Join a softball team, volleyball team, bowling league, or crafts group. Share in the fellowship. Stretch yourself to be more vulnerable. Risk in doing something frivolous and fun. Challenge yourself. Succeed in a project and feel proud. Or, fail gloriously and feel humbled and child-like, but happy that you tried. Exhaust yourself with exercise, then glory in a wonderful steamy shower and a good night's sleep between freshly laundered sheets.

Diet is also very important. Avoid fatty, heavily sugared, and junk foods. Eat plenty of fresh fruits and vegetables. Eat in moderation. Stay away from stimulants and depressants. That means avoiding caffeine, nicotine, and alcohol. Particularly beware of marijuana or other mind altering drugs. These put your spirit into a deeper slumber than ever before.

❧ Read good Christian literature to help you focus on self discovery, personal devotions, and inspiration.

Bookstores and libraries stock a wealth of good books from which to choose, ranging from religious classics to contemporary poetry and inspirational works. Discover the richness of biographies of great Christian leaders in history. Explore Christian family values and challenge yourself to define a personal ethical stance.

Participate in guided Bible study, focusing on the ways God could be speaking to you through the Scripture. Avoid fastening onto the "shoulds" and the "oughts" that tighten you into striving. See and celebrate the very real passions and emotions of biblical characters.

Write down meaningful quotes you come across. Stick them on your refrigerator or bulletin board. Let them become a part of your life. Share good ideas and inspirational thoughts with friends.

Express yourself. Keep a journal to jot down your thoughts and prayers daily. Write your own brief psalms of praise for the little things in life that give you pleasure and for which you can thank God. Celebrate good ideas that inspire you.

❧ Get involved in nature, music and art.

Large doses of nature are a tonic to the spirit. Get outside and take walks in the park or the woods. Go camping or fishing.

Walk along the seashore and hunt for shells or driftwood. Go out at night and study the stars. Pay attention to the beauty of sunrises and sunsets. Experience how big and how wonderful God's creation is.

Listen to good music that will relax you, stimulate your imagination, or inspire you spiritually.

Also, surround yourself with good art. Spend time in museums, art galleries, or viewing art books that will awaken your creative interests.

❦ Touch others and allow yourself to be touched in Christian love and fellowship.

Practice making eye-to-eye contact whenever you talk to other people. Don't be afraid to take another person's hand, touch them in friendship on the arm or shoulder, hug them in greeting or in saying good bye. Encourage group togetherness by physically touching each other in times of prayer. Bless each other with the laying on of hands.

Hug your children, even though it may feel awkward to you or perhaps you have felt that they are too old for that kind of expression. Put your arm around them while walking or talking. Relax and express yourself to them physically.

Be honest with yourself about your thoughts and feelings. Discern in your own mind the difference between sexual attraction and wholesome expressions of love and friendship. Ask Jesus to take the lust from your struggling mind and put it to death on the cross so that you might enter into relationships with pure motives and without the baggage of hidden sexual agendas.

Face up to your sexual vulnerability and let God help you overcome temptation through prayer. Pray for the transformation of your mind and emotions into wholesome thoughts and feelings about physical contact.

❦ Get involved in helping others.

Don't just focus on your own needs. Learn to give as well as take. If you want others to be there for you, then be willing to be there for them. Stay aware. Ministry to others in need will do much to help you rethink the priorities in your own life, and to put your needs in proper perspective. The only danger here is if you escape into a total focus on other people's needs and do not tend to your own spirit awakening.

❦ Pray for your own healing.

Ask your inner child to forgive those who did not give you nurture. Pray for your heart of stone to be softened.

Pray to be released from your inner vows that shield you from being vulnerable to others. Trust that the pain of being more open will bring rich rewards of friendship and renewed trust.

Pray for the Holy Spirit to guide you on a journey of new discovery, to be able to come awake to the simple joys of life and to the wonder of deepened personal relationships.

Pray for others and ask them to pray for you. Pray with confidence that God has the power to transform you and that through the cross of Jesus Christ you will overcome all difficulties. Pray that your spirit will come alive in new awareness and new vitality.

Talk to God at every opportunity through flash prayers throughout the day. Develop an attitude of prayer. Listen to what God may be saying to you in return.

Pay attention to your dreams which are unusually vivid or come repeatedly. Pray that you may understand what they mean and be able to hear God's messages.

Start each day with an "out loud" prayer in which you enthusiastically choose life, openness, relationships, love, vibrancy, and fun. If indeed we are what we think, then make your thought patterns for the day a prayer of positive affirmations to God. Tell yourself and God that you will think and behave in ways which exemplify a fully awakened personal spirit.

Pay whatever price of self-discipline, trust, vulnerability, and personal pain that is necessary in order to come alive.

Jesus said

He came to give us life,

and that more abundantly.

Seek it!

❦ Lord, give me the courage to break out of familiar patterns and to try new resources for refreshment and growth. Help me to let go of rigid over-burdening seriousness.

Teach me to play so that the child in me has an opportunity to thrive.

Enable me to choose life continually, in my prayer discipline and in my attitude and actions toward myself and others.

Give me the strength of spirit to take the initiative to reach out to people — to let them know and minister to me, as well as to make myself available to know and to minister to them.

Help me to live in the joy of Your loving grace.

Life Applications:
Rise and Shine: Re-Awakening Your Spirit

1. Review the questions you asked yourself on page 115 that *"explore ways in which your spirit may be asleep."* Discuss with your group or a friend the areas in which you need the most rejuvenation.

2. Think through and write out a personal plan of spiritual renewal by describing actions you will take for each of the following suggestions. Be sure you take action in each area at least once a week.

Seek affection in my own family.
I will:

Seek out a small group of Christian friends who can understand, support and confront me in love.
I will:

Seek ways to lighten my heart through fun.
I will:

Take care of myself through sleep, exercise, and diet.
I will:

Read good Christian devotional literature.
I will:

Get involved in nature, music, and art.
I will:

Touch and be touched in Christian fellowship.
I will:

Get involved in helping others.
I will:

Pray for my own inner healing.
I will:

Consider how each of the actions you have listed can be worked into your weekly and daily schedule. Actually put them on your calendar as a daily reminder to seek these ways to awaken your spirit.

Chapter 8
Nurture through Family, Friends, and Small Groups

Never so lonely as on this day.
The sun hanging cold against a white sky.
Only the horizon rimmed with gold.
An omen of life distant from me.
Cold from the rain of yesterday
I trudged with head bowed.
Seeking solitude
I pushed against the chill
Hurrying toward the nothingness
Of my busy day.
Then you.
Suddenly there.
An insult to my isolation.
With laughing face you stunned me
With unavoidable presence.
Love, hope, joy, encounter
Leaped out at me
And sent me reeling.
And I was afraid—
Not of you,
But of myself and who I had become.
Your gentle Christian joy
Slapped me in the face
And waked a consciousness
Of life unborn within me.
I had felt only the cold.
I had not raised my head
To see the promise of the sky.
I had allowed my spirit to burn low and die.

Then you, with laughing face.
Unexpectedly.
Thanks for being filled,
For being God's person,
For doing God's work.
Thanks for shocking me alive
With your happy laughing face.
With your lively Christian grace.

— Norm Bowman

There are two kinds of families which we consider to be very important in waking the slumbering spirit: **Our natural families** into which we were born, and the **family of God** through which we share a kinship through faith in Jesus Christ. We have said much about the importance of the natural family assuming God-intended responsibility for spiritual nurture which produces fully human men and women. That nurturing is essentially accomplished, or not accomplished, in the early years of a child's life.

If a natural family imparts love, affection, touching, and spiritual nurture, the natural and effervescent personal spirit within children can be kept alive as they grow into adulthood. If however, the spirit fails to be nurtured, or later falls into a slumbering state through sin, neglect of worship, or the seduction of a spiritually impoverished lifestyle, awakening must come through the help of friends who can re-nurture one back to life.

Family members or friends cannot shake someone awake any more than a sinner can be harassed into contrition. Slumbering spirits do not need scolding, criticism or advice.

Awareness and choice to seek an awakening must come from within a person. It is best encouraged by identifying with a gentle, loving, fun-filled community of friends.

If family members are also slumbering in their spirits and are unaware, then the extended family of God must assume the role as nurturing agents to bring about awakening.

This is not a quick and easy process and should not be expected to come as an instant miracle of transformation. Awakening cannot be accomplished solely by others for us; it requires our own determination, bolstered by continuous love and encouragement of others. Friends and family need to recognize that waking the slumbering spirit will most often be a long journey with two steps forward and one step back. It will be a journey with many confusing branches in the road and much fog to obscure the vision. But it is a journey of infinite worth for both the pilgrim and the guides.

For an adult coming into the realization of one's slumbering spirit, the best source of help is through the loving nurture of a small group. Every Christian congregation should have cell groups dedicated to Bible study, prayer, inner healing, and service projects which direct their energies outward.

Small groups are where "church" really happens because that is where the work of Christ is done in the world. Small groups are where God becomes incarnate through love. Small groups allow the power of the Holy Spirit to work in true corporateness where the grace of God comes alive and is applied to the lives of people to heal wounds caused by sin and neglect.

There is no greater gift a family member or a friend can bestow than to involve a loved one in a small group which can love him back to life. Groups will be imperfect, and not every group will be the right fit. But it is worth the search to find the right combination of Christian people to administer the rejuvenation of God's grace.

Guidelines to help Christian small groups reach their healing potential

1. Establish a regular meeting time and expectation of attendance.

Relationship building requires presence, both physically and emotionally. If a group is to be productive it must meet regularly enough for members to gain weekly sustenance from each other and to have a sense from day to day about what is going on in the lives of those involved.

It is essential for a group to make a real commitment about certain ground rules. The first of these should be a commitment to be present whenever possible and to come, not as an observer, but with willingness to share from one's heart.

Meet at the same place for the first six weeks or so to enhance the group's bonding. Share the expense of hiring a teenager to look after the children while you meet. Or, you could rotate childcare among group members by dropping off children at one location and taking turns.

Atmosphere at group meetings can be very important. Bright lights and big rooms are not conducive to sharing. Find an agreeable meeting place which is quiet, free from distractions, and which has a feeling of intimacy. A home is ideal if it can be free from the telephone ringing and the children interrupting.

If you must meet in a church classroom, go to one corner, put down a throw rug, plug in a floor lamp, and turn off the overhead lights. Also be sure to sit close to each other to create a feeling of togetherness and so everyone can be seen and heard.

2. Select a competent leader/facilitator for best results.

Total spontaneity and shared leadership in small groups is not without successful precedent. However, if a recognized leader is available to facilitate the process, the group is much more likely to stay focused, on track, productive, and happy.

The ideal facilitator, of course, would be a trained counselor, experienced in group dynamics, familiar with the principles of inner healing, and having the confidence of all group members. But few groups will have the good fortune of such enlightened leadership.

If a group gets stuck on single issues, seems always out of control, or is inconsistent and inattentive to evident needs, it is probably a sign of lack of leadership.

A minimum requirement for a successful group is to choose the person best equipped from among the members who can serve as an organizer or shepherd to make arrangements, facilitate the program, and direct the sharing time to keep the group as focused and constructive as possible. A good leader is one who can comfortably share from his or her own life and who is interested in and respectful of the participation of everyone in the group.

Group leadership may be shared—with each member exercising his best gifts to provide administration, hospitality, music, teaching, wise counsel, or special kinds of ministry. Whatever is done, the group should focus on helping each member to be his or her best self and to gain the maximum benefit from the time spent together.

Lay leadership can be very effective in most group settings. However, there are types of problems among potential group members that should not be dealt with unless under the leadership of a trained professional counselor.

Group members should recognize that alcoholism, drug addiction, sexual abuse, and physical abuse are hard issues which require special care and training. Lay-person-led small groups should not undertake the task of providing major kinds of therapy related to problems which should be dealt with in professional counseling. Otherwise, the group will become too focused on extreme situations it cannot adequately handle and

which rob others with lesser needs of the opportunity for healing and growth.

3. Include a time of worship and a time of singing.

Group time should always include a time of inspiration and
fun, a time to be renewed in fellowship and to charge one's spiritual batteries. Devotional worship and sharing through song is
an excellent way to maintain that focus. Worship and song also
prepare everyone's spirit to hear messages from God and to be
tuned in to the spirits of others in the group.

Groups can also profit by planning times which are designed
for pure recreation. Picnics, outings, concerts and other events
held for the fun of getting together provide the relaxed fellowship that will help group members to bond in different ways.
These events are a good time to establish relationships with the
families of other members so you can all know and understand
each other on a deeper level.

4. Conduct some kind of objective study on an appropriate topic that will both interest and inform group members.

The infusion of fresh, new, and well-honed ideas through a
time of study will keep the group from focusing exclusively on
the heavy issues of its own members' needs. However, be careful so as not to get overly caught up in the study and flee into
the "safe objectivity" of it to avoid dealing with needed personal
issues. Times of Bible study or of book study should contribute
to the sharing and healing process but cannot be a substitute for it.

If a study is undertaken, the leader should always be careful
to call for personal application of the ideas presented. He or she
should always challenge the group to consider how ideas can be
translated to action:

♦ How can this idea make a difference in my life?

♦ How can I apply this to solve a problem, heal a hurt, or to awaken my slumbering spirit?

5. Be honest and real in group relationships.

Open and honest discussion of life concerns is essential if a small group is to succeed. Unless group members are accustomed to sharing from the heart, it may be difficult for them to do anything but make easy conversation about issues of no consequence. Or, some individuals may be willing to deal with issues other people share, but they are reluctant at first to speak up and reveal their own needs and concerns.

For group members to warm up to one another, it is best to start sharing with simple, open requests to which everyone can respond. For example: "Tell me about one of your fondest childhood memories." Or perhaps: "Describe the person and the place that represented the center of emotional warmth to you while growing up."

From there you can move on to deeper and perhaps more painful issues which could be dealt with in a healing way by the group.

If nobody else in the group is sharing from their heart, take the lead and say, "Let me tell you what my story is, and my problems. I want you to pray for me."

Usually when one person starts, it just breaks open like a flood and others will share. Once people learn that the group is a safe place to share, they will participate with growing enthusiasm. More and more they will want to open up and share with real honesty what is going on inside them.

6. Be open to new people coming into the group.

Although effective groups are built around people who have learned (oftentimes through struggle) to relate well to each other and are willing to be there for mutual support, avoid shutting new members out. The concept of a group that grows like a cell, continually giving birth to other groups, is a healthy model to emulate. A group can become too closed, too much of a clique, and too inbred to continue vibrant growth among its members. It is almost always very healthy to bring new people into the group relationships.

We've been in several groups where once that basic trust of openness and sharing was established, new people could come into the group without deterring the old members from sharing, and once the new people saw what was happening, they would immediately be open as well. It is amazing how quickly that happens.

Research has shown that when a group grows to twelve or more people, the usual problems of group dynamics begin to happen—a few do all the talking. Groups should have an apprentice facilitator who can learn and practice various group dynamic skills. Then, leadership is available when it is time for the parent group to birth a second group. Smaller groups are more manageable, more productive, and are able to openly welcome new members.

Particularly within the church family, the occasional rotation of members between various share groups will create a healthy unity within the diversity and promote sharing throughout the congregation.

Lyman Coleman, author, lecturer, and creator of the well known *Serendipity* small group movement, teaches that groups need to discover a purpose beyond themselves within a year of their organization. If groups do not get into ministry of some sort, or parent another group and welcome new members, they tend to become dysfunctional. Coleman frequently uses the technique of placing an empty chair at group meetings. This is a purposeful reminder to members that they need to reach out to others and bring them in to benefit from the healing and growth that can come through small group relationships. Small groups can accomplish healing, ministry, and evangelism at its very best.

7. Stay aware of possible discomfort in group dynamics.

Recognize that some group members will have very strong needs to be met and will require and even demand a lot of attention. This can cause a discomfort level for others. When people have been raised in very dysfunctional families, they will seek answers to their needs in whatever kind of small group they find.

If the group is enlightened about how the personal spirit can slumber, they will more easily recognize what is going on when a person objectifies or projects a lot of the angers and frustrations they have onto certain people within the group. When this happens, group members don't have to take it as a personal offense and react. They can recognize that the person needs some unconditional love and they can give it.

Certain "shame" issues also may be present among group members. This is often the case with victims of incest, sexual or physical abuse, homosexuality, or adult children of alcoholics. To deal with these particularly sensitive areas, the group may have to agree within itself on a boundary system to establish rules of how far to probe, and a referral system to handle crises.

Members should come into the group recognizing that it will not be all pleasant fellowship and light-hearted good times. There may be honest hurts and angers expressed and confrontations needed. The group may not be fully competent to handle every situation and may need to recommend one-on-one professional counseling. Love is the key. The group must hang together in loving commitment and be willing to work through the rough times to accomplish healing.

8. Don't be afraid to establish needed boundaries.

Occasionally a person who has wanted parenting and has never received it may tend to latch onto a mother or father figure within the church or the small group and consequently ask too much of them. This kind of overwhelming need may become very demanding.

The spiritual mother-and-father-figures may feel like they are being eaten alive and should set boundaries for their own emotional protection. If some parameters are to be drawn, simply say "I care about you and want to spend time with you, but your need for attention is inordinate. I can't allow you to occupy all my time, as I wouldn't for one of my natural children." The group member hungry for spiritual parenting must learn through verbal teaching how to be appropriate in the search for meaningful nurture.

9. Respect the confidentiality of what is shared in groups.

In order to share with others from their hearts, group members want to be able to trust that their confessions and expressions of need will be held in confidence by others and not be discussed outside the group.

The only exception to this might be in the discovery of sexual or physical abuse. In such cases there is a legal and moral responsibility to take whatever action is needed to prevent further endangerment of the victim, particularly if children are involved. Groups should act with Christian grace to provide comfort, counsel, and protection for the abused and find professional help for the abuser.

10. Recognize that true healing is not accomplished by our doing, but by God's Holy Spirit, working through His church, facilitated through prayer.

Change in a person's life cannot happen without an acknowledgment of need and a desire to be different. However, recognition of a wounded and slumbering spirit does not assure that healing will happen. Many people stay in private therapy for years and become very enlightened about their psychological state. But healing is not accomplished without the grace of forgiveness and the transformation of the inner person through the presence of the Holy Spirit.

Christians forming small groups for the purpose of healing wounds, waking slumbering spirits, and sustaining each other in love, must recognize that they have the power of the church. It is not their power. It is the power of God incarnate in them through the Holy Spirit who can work miracles of love in the lives of people.

Prayer is essential. Prayer is the way in which God and man are joined in open communication and through which the healing power of God pours out through loving relationships among Christian friends.

Small groups literally can love a slumbering spirit back to life—not by their own power, for it is God who does it through them. Prayer and re-nurturing love are the dynamic forces through which healing and spiritual awakening are accomplished.

11. Recognize and celebrate growth among group members.

As real personal growth begins to happen, group members need to recognize how individuals are coming alive and acknowledge their growth openly through affirmations, compliments, and encouragement. The group can celebrate the unfolding of rejuvenated personal spirits and share as a group in that joy.

"The creation waits in eager anticipation for the sons of God to be revealed." (Romans 9: 19)

"Let us hold unswervingly to the hope we profess, for He who promised is faithful. And let us consider how we may spur one another on toward love and good deeds." (Hebrews 10: 23-24)

12. Exhibit Fruits of the Spirit and do not fear moving on to new relationships.

In all that you do, keep in mind those basic life-principles that Paul described as the fruits of God's Spirit working in you. As you relate to each other to accomplish inner healing and awaken the slumbering spirit, you can do no better than to care for each other in:

♦ Love
♦ Joy
♦ Peace
♦ Patience
♦ Kindness
♦ Goodness
♦ Faithfulness
♦ Gentleness
♦ Self-Control

When a group is truly bonded in love and support, there will come a time when members move from sharing their own stories to a higher and more intimate plane —creating the group's own unique story by becoming a community. True community evokes wonderful feelings of joy and security which we may be tempted to grasp too tightly for fear they will slip away.

Yet the amazing dynamic of real community among persons with awakened personal spirits is that the accompanying catharsis and bonding allow them to release each other to move on to new places and new experiences and to maturity in Christ. (Ephesians 4: 11-16)

Do not be fearful of leaving behind a small group of dear supportive friends who have helped you to become more fully human. The bonding of past relationships is never lost. As Lyman Coleman says, bonded relationships continue to function "on call" for a lifetime. Everyone then has the freedom to build an ever-widening circle of friends with whom to share love and nurture for a richer and more fulfilling life.

Heavenly **Father**, thank You for the good and positive things my earthly parents have given me. Thank You also that I never have to be stuck with the negative and hurtful experiences of my life. I don't have to make do with a starvation diet, or a twisted and distorted image of who I am. Jesus can make all things new.

Increase the glory of my new birth in You. I want to be fully free and alive in the family of God where Jesus can have opportunity to love and heal and nurture me through relationships with mothers and fathers, sisters and brothers, grandparents, aunts, uncles and cousins in the Lord.

I want to be fully a part of Your family, Lord—rooted in love, and growing in every way to become all that You have created me to be.

I trust You, Lord, to love others to fullness of life through me. Help me never to focus on the imperfections of those around me, but rather always to focus on You—beginning a good work in me today and surely perfecting it until the day of Christ Jesus.

Life Applications:
Nurture through Family,
Friends, and Small Groups

1 . Do you feel a need to be a member of a small group of Christians who can provide nurture for you? If so, identify the three most basic needs that you would like a group to fulfill.

2. Identify three contributions you believe you could bring to a group to help make it an effective healing environment for you and for others.

3. Describe a time in your life when you felt the most involved, loved, happy, and spiritually fulfilled.

4. What were the most important elements that contributed to those good feelings?

5. Seriously consider these questions and jot down your ideas:

♦ What would it take to create the proper kind of environment in which to grow spiritually in my life today?

♦ What kind of persons should I seek?

♦ Where should I seek them?

♦ What will I have to do to help stimulate the kind of nurturing I need?

6. Discuss these issues with a friend, or with the group you are in already. Then write out a personal plan of action to which you are willing to commit yourself.

Actions I will take to seek nurturing friendships:

Places I will go to find the right kind of friends:

Actions I will take to stimulate my own nurtured growth and spirit awakening:

7. Review your plan of action once a month. Check yourself to determine whether you are remaining "on course." Are you keeping your commitments to yourself? If not, why not?

The Rest of the Story

We all can use a reminder occasionally that some things are not what they at first appear to be — and when we get caught up in foolishness (or just plain being wrong), the best medicine is confession.

We began this book with a story about a wild kitten born in the garage to a wild mother named Fraidie. That kitten, through loving nurture, became the snugly and warm family pet named Lady. The story we told is perfectly true, as is the analogy that each of us needs a similar kind of loving nurture to come into our full humanity with an awakened personal spirit. But we cannot let that story end without confessing a later development which has humbled us, left us laughing at ourselves, and taught another object lesson as well.

Cat lovers will usually admit there is something special about a sweet little girl kitten that makes you feel differently than you do about a "tomcat." That's the way we were feeling about Lady. She was so affectionate and frisky. It was so cute how she had learned to jump up on our bed in the mornings to wake us by pushing her head beneath our hands, asking to be petted to start her day and ours.

When she was about six months old, she went through a period of about three days in which she began acting rather strange and agitated. We thought at first that she was just bridging her adolescence and was experiencing her first period of being in heat. But this particular morning, as we were ruffling her soft fur there on the bed, we had quite a surprise. We discovered that this sweet little girl kitten was not a lady at all. Virtually overnight, in what appeared to be some latent gland development, Lady produced the unmistakable evidence that she was really a teenage Tom!

Our first response was: "This is unbelievable!" Then, "How embarrassing!" Finally: "How will we muster the nerve to tell our friends that we can't tell the difference between a male and a female cat?"

After half a day of shaking our heads in shock and self-doubt, we regained some composure by remembering that this kitten had been to the vet to get an exam and the usual series of shots. If the vet hadn't questioned why we would name a boy kitten Lady, then maybe he was confused too. Why should we feel so bad?

That afternoon, Lady was renamed Grady. During the next few days a rather remarkable thing began to happen. We started thinking of Grady in new ways. Yes, he was still the sweet, cuddly, frisky and affectionate kitten we had known as Lady. But he somehow seemed less feminine now that we knew he was not a female. We began to play with him differently. Instead of thinking of him as a cute and coy little girl, we began to call him a "little rascal"—a decidedly masculine perception.

"Isn't that strange?" we commented. And then with a little deeper thought we wondered aloud: "Maybe that's more of a comment on us than it is on Grady, who after all was just being his same sweet self!"

If the Fraidie-Lady analogy holds true to illustrate the power of loving nurture, then perhaps the Lady-Grady episode can teach us something as well. Maybe the end result of nurture is determined in large measure by how one is perceived by others, and how one ultimately comes to perceive one's self.

Did Grady become a sweet and loving cat because we treated him as a kitten like we perceived him (or her) to be? If we had initially perceived him to be a Tom and had treated him more rough-and-tumble, or perhaps more distantly macho, would he have turned out differently? Probably!

We can learn lessons here on several levels: First, we should carefully evaluate how we perceive and treat children. For example, do we automatically go into auto pilot to raise girls as sweeties and boys as toughies? Or, can we appreciate strength in women and tenderness in men and allow these qualities to develop naturally in children no matter what their gender?

It is likely that children will rise to the highest level of our expectations if we love them properly, give them room to learn and grow, and consistently administer God's grace.

Secondly, do we recognize in ourselves how the nurturing environment in which we have lived has done much to produce our own self-concept? Do we recognize the extent to which the perceptions we have of ourselves were shaped by the treatment and attitudes of others? Have we gone to sleep spiritually, not of our own choosing, but out of inadequate nurture, neglect, and our own lack of understanding how to stay fully alive?

Most importantly, do we know how to get beyond those limitations to begin to grow instead into who God wants us to be as our best selves? Do we understand how important it is to find Christian friends who will love, nurture and encourage? Do we understand how God desires for us to be fully awake, sensitive to His voice, and responsive to His Spirit in our lives?

If there is but one lingering message that should be understood by reading this book, it is that you do not have to live your life as a victim.

No matter what your journey has been;
no matter what nurturing
or lack of nurturing you have experienced;
no matter what pain and scars you bear—
from this moment on,
life is a choosing.

Rise and shine, you sleeping spirits! Like Grady the wild kitten who now so dearly loves the stroking hand, do not fear asking for affection that will nourish and refresh. Venture out into new territories, secure in the protection of a God who loves you and will surely be your guide. 🐾

Suggestions for Further Reading

Berg, Elizabeth. *Family Traditions, Celebrations for Holidays and Everyday.* Pleasantville, NY, The Reader's Digest Association, Inc., 1992.

Coleman, Lyman. *Serendipity Small Group Training Manual.* Box 1012, Littleton, CO 80160, Serendipity House, 1991.

Faber, Adele and Mazlish, Elaine. *How to Talk So Kids Will Listen & Listen So Kids Will Talk.* New York, Avon, 1990

Edelman, Marian Wright. *The Measure of Our Success. Boston,* Beacon Press, 1992.

Fitzpatrick, Jean Grasso. *Something More, Nurturing Your Child's Spiritual Growth.* New York, Viking, 1991.

Sandford, John & Paula. *Healing the Wounded Spirit.* Tulsa, Victory House, Inc., 1985.

Sullivan, S. Adams. *The Quality Time Almanac, A Sourcebook of Ideas and Activities for Parents and Kids.* Garden City, New York, Doubleday & Company, Inc., 1986.

Swindoll, Charles R. *The Grace Awakening.* Dallas, Word Publishing, 1990.

Glossary of common terms
as used in this book

Noah Webster worked diligently for over thirty years to assemble the dictionary which we generally accept as the standard for academic use today. Putting together a universally acceptable dictionary of theological terms would perhaps be even more difficult. We know this glossary certainly will not satisfy everyone with its choice of words, denominational orthodoxy, or comprehensiveness of definitions. Our intention is to help readers understand in a very basic way some of the key theological terms used in this book. Please accept it for what it is and read with Christian grace.

Body — The flesh and blood of one's earthly form, spiritually linked as the dwelling place (temple) of one's mind, soul, and personal spirit.

Body of Christ — The Church universal including all persons who have confessed that Jesus Christ is the Son of God and have committed to follow him as their Lord and Savior.

Born Again — A term describing one who has repented of sin, received the forgiving grace of Jesus Christ, and attempts to walk in newness of life through the power of His death, burial, and resurrection.

Charismatic — A born again Christian who recognizes and personally utilizes the unique gifts of God's Holy Spirit with which he or she is equipped to do the work of Christ in the world for the edification of Christ's Church.

Church — All those who confess Jesus as Christ, the Messiah, Son of the one true God, and who join together in fellowship to do God's work.

Conscience — A *true conscience* is activated through an awakened personal spirit to allow one to empathize with the possible hurt to another person or one's self. It provides warning ahead of time to avoid actions that will cause hurt or injustice. A *remorse conscience* works after an event as a reminder of wrongs committed. It is activated primarily on the basis of rules or laws broken, or on regret for having been caught — not out of empathy for one who might have been hurt by one's actions.

Evangelical —Persons who know, have experienced and teach what it is to be born again in Jesus Christ.

Family of God — All persons, whether blood relatives or not, who consciously contribute to the spiritual nurture of others out of the love and unity they feel as followers of Jesus Christ.

Holy Spirit — The spiritual presence of God, who is three in one (Father, Son, and Holy Spirit) who dwells among us to convict us of sin, call us into repentence and salvation, comfort us in need, and empower us to do His work in the world.

Human Animal — By purely scientific definition, humans are animals which fit the classification of mammals since they are warm blooded, produce milk to feed offspring born alive, and have bodily hair. The human animal, however, is uniquely distinguished from other animals by virtue of the human mind (logical reasoning intellect), the personal spirit (God-given life force which can achieve intimate communication and relationships with others and with God), and the soul (the capacity of the personal spirit to encounter life, react, and build character and personality).

Human —To have an awakened personal spirit by which we identify and empathize with others, becoming one with them, and cherishing what is in the other person even more than our own life. In short, being fully human is to be like Jesus.

Humanism — The glorification of the human position, placing man as the crown of the universe, becoming ever more elevated in intellect and relationships based on his rational thought and good works. Humanism stands as an imitation of what God, the Creator and sustainer of all life, is doing to transform men and women into the character of Jesus Christ through His saving grace.

Incarnation —The act of God in which He actually became human flesh through Jesus Christ that all persons might be brought into restored relationship with Him. Persons share in the incarnation as they profess Jesus Christ as Savior and allow God's Holy Spirit to take control of their lives to do the work of Christ in the world.

Inner Healing — The healing of spiritual and emotional wounds resulting in renewed inner peace and the restoration of right relationships with others and with God. Inner healing is accomplished by acknowledging one's sins and woundings, repentently taking needs to God in prayer, forgiving others, and accepting forgiveness. The transforming power of Christ makes all things new by taking the sin and woundings of mankind upon Himself.

Inspiration — Creative concepts, ideas, insights, understandings, or expressions of feeling which are communicated by God's Spirit through an individual's awakened personal spirit.

Keys of Knowledge — Special insights given by God to help persons understand their spiritual condition and to be able to seek inner healing and spiritual restoration through His grace.

Mind — Our intellect, the reasoning and logical decision-making capacity to choose a course of action.

Nurture — The cumulative effect of how one loves, cares for, teaches, and sets an example in the shaping of another person's personal spirit, thoughts, feelings, and character.

Personal Spirit — The God-given life force within an individual that determines how one relates to others and to God, and how vibrancy of life and quality of soul are developed and maintained.

Prayer — Personal communication with God for the purpose of praise, thanksgiving, seeking help, or to intercede for the benefit of others with whom one identifies.

Prophet — One who has a specific gift from God's Holy Spirit to understand and communicate God's Word with power, conviction, and clarity.

Religion — The form or ritual of worship and devotion to God which can be involved in true spirit to Spirit relationship with God, but often is focused on rules, regulations, rituals and customs.

Slumbering Spirit — One who through lack of proper nurture as a child has been stunted in his or her ability to relate adequately to others and to God; or who, as an adult, has withdrawn from intimate relationships, withdrawn from art and nature, neglected worship, and fallen into repeated sin, resulting in spiritual and emotional lethargy.

Soul —That structure of the mind, character, and personality which is developed as one's personal spirit encounters life, reacts, and builds coping mechanisms.

Speaking in Tongues — One of many gifts of God's Holy Spirit, enabling the receipient to praise God or to receive a message from God, spirit to Spirit, in a way which circumvents the language patterns or limiting filters of one's conscious mind.

Spiritual Gifts — God's special gifts of enabling power through His Holy Spirit by which Christians are equipped to do the work of Christ in the world for the development of His Church.

Worship — An attitude of reverence, awe, thankfulness, self giving, vulnerability, communication, and joyous praise of God, made possible by the inspiration of God's Holy Spirit and our openness to His presence.

Materials available through Elijah House

Books
John Sandford and Paula Sandford
The Elijah Task
Restoring the Christian Family
The Transformation of the Inner Man
Healing the Wounded Spirit

John Sandford
Why Some Christians Commit Adultery

Paula Sandford
Healing Victims of Sexual Abuse
Healing Women's Emotions

John Sandford and Loren Sandford
The Renewal of the Mind

John Sandford and Mark Sandford
Deliverance and Inner Healing

Loren Sandford
Wounded Warriors — Surviving Seasons of Stress
Divine Doctoring of Small Groups

Video and Audio Tapes
John and Paula Sandford
The Relationship Series — Set of four video tapes.

Numerous other titles. Write or call for a catalog.

Elijah House, Inc.
S. 1000 Richards Road
Post Falls, Idaho 83854
Phone (208) 773-1645

For quantity discounts on the purchase of this book, contact the publisher.
Clear Stream, Inc.
Box 122128
Arlington, TX 76012